MW01195872

THE

CATHAR

DIALOGUES

THE

CATHAR

DIALOGUES

Betwixt
Henri de Nebours
and
Guillaume de Mirepoix.

Recounted by
Johny Bineham

Al cap des set ans vedrego le laurel

Dedicated to Melva.
Many have lived together,
but not too many
have been burnt together.

The
Cathar
Dialogues

Copyright © Johny Bineham, 2009.

This book is in copyright. Subject to statuary exceptions
and to the provisions of relevant collective licencing
agreements. No reproduction may take place without
the written agreement of Johny Bineham,

Johny Bineham, Sydney, New South Wales,
Australia.

ISBN 13: 978-1496006356
ISBN 10: 1496006356

First published 2009

Al cap des set ans vedrego le laurel

Contents

Please Note.

The Cathar Dialogues and *A Cathar Gnostic Codex,* though books in their own right, are in effect, one book divided into two for convenience sake.

The Cathar Dialogues relate the total experience, whereas *A Cathar Codex* is designed as a reference, as a summation of *The Cathar Dialogues.*

Foreward

The literary world is generally aware of the Cathars through the horrors of the Albigensian Crusade and the many massacres of the Cathar *Perfecti*. The subsequent final annihilation of Medieval Dualistic Gnostic Catharism by the horrors of the Inquisition has forever stained with blood, sword and fire, the honour of the Catholic Church. Though the Inquisition was diabolically effective in physically liquidating them, yet many of their beliefs as well as an awareness of their goodness are reemerging worldwide.

The Inquisition in their quest to obliterate every last Cathar, had thousands of *Perfecti* and their *credente* (lay followers) burnt at the stake. The ashes however, of these victims of religious intolerance are akin to the Arabian phoenix arising afresh after some seven hundred years from those mounds of cinders long since scattered to the four winds. Bodies and minds may be religiously burnt to a crisp, yet ideas, ideals and aspirations, are far more difficult to eradicate.

This publication is an actual account of the 'dialogues' between Henri de Nebours and Guillaume de Mirepoix, The conversations set down herein could be considered as informed insights into the mind of a learned Cathar *Perfecti*.

There are many paths leading to the acquisition of past and present learning, for example these 'dialogues'. Henri de Nebours posited the question to the book-loving Guillaume de Mirepoix when he first made his presence felt and heard, "Do you think all knowledge comes from books?"

The Cathar *Perfecti*, as with any other group under continuing instruction, were of varying levels of spiritual and mystical education. Luckily for us, Henri de Nebours was well versed in Cathar knowledge and highly tutored in Cathar philosophy.

Most dates of the discussions are precise, while the others are encompassed within a period of time. All entries are in sequence. Some small sections of *The Cathar Dialogues* have been omitted, being of a very personal nature. Other information was meant as instructions for those who are well advanced along the Path and so are also omitted. There are no explanatory notes, as The 'Dialogues' are sufficient of themselves.

These 'Dialogues' are, as Henri said, "A Crusade for the few, not the multitude." for the world has more than sufficient religions and doctrines without adding to them. Nevertheless, *The Cathar Dialogues* do hope to demonstrate the relevance of evolved Cathar Gnostic philosophic thought for contemporary times.

Certainly, a reason for publishing *The Cathar Dialogues* was to dispel for some, that Catharism was a dour, pessimistic belief system. All groups have their fair share of both pessimists and optimists within their ranks. It is also true, that among of the vast array of differing Gnostic sects, some philosophies were indeed pessimistic, such as believing that it was pointless to procreate, for it would entrap the offspring in the harsh and vicious materialistic world of that era. Medieval Dualistic Gnostic Catharism, however, was the most evolved and optimistic of all Gnostic traditions. Certainly, not 'pessimistic' and 'without hope' as Steven Runciman commented in the final chapter of his otherwise erudite book, *The Medieval Manichee*:

It was not an ignoble religion. It taught the value of the fundamental virtues; it faced with courage the anxious question of evil. But it was a religion of pessimism, it held out no hope for individual men and their salvation. Mankind should die out, that the imprisoned fragments of Godhead could return to their home. It was a religion without hope and such a religion cannot survive unless it is helped artificially.

The above concept is refuted on the basis that the Cathar core belief was that each Divine Spark (each person's essential eternal essence, the innermost core of their being) will ultimately be reunited with the Divine Source, bypassing the God of the Great Faiths, as well as any extreme punishments such as one's possible eternal punishment in hell.

Surely, this ultimate blissful reunion for all, namely, the reunification of the Divine Spark with The Source, must make it in reality, the most optimistic of all belief systems. With Catharism there was no heavenly salvation to strive for during the one allotted lifetime, nor any eternal damnation to fear at the end of it. Actually, it would be a sad day for psychiatrists if all of us became either 'true' Gnostics or Cathars.

It is certainly true that the Cathars considered the salvation of the soul irrelevant, for they were only concerned with the return of the Divine Spark to The Source, all else was pointless. Consequently, the Cathar *Perfecti*, when hauled before the Inquisition were happy to answer either 'yes' or 'no', to any charges put to them. The Inquisition's questions, as well as the Cathar's answers, were as illusory and transient as most everything else is in this world of matter.

They did not believe in oaths, therefore, did not swear them. The swearing of oaths (of allegiance, etc) was a major pivotal aspect of the feudal medieval world. Consequently, for the meticulously pedantic Inquisitors who precisely recorded every interrogation, the *Perfecti* answers must have been a real pain in the butt, as well as leaving a quagmire of mis- and disinformation for future historians.

The educated evolved Cathar cleric believed that The Source (not the Artificer, which is the God of the Great Faiths) created each and every person's Divine Spark which would ultimately be drawn back to The Source. This may take many, many lifetimes over aeons before the soul aspect of our existence was sufficiently enlightened for reunion.

Also, with the gift of creation for every Divine Spark, there came the accompanying gift of immortality for eternity. So, looking at the rather lengthy extra-large picture of eternity for everyone, what if it did take few hundred, or indeed a few thousand lifetimes to finally acquire the spiritual knowledge and the mystical *gnosis* necessary to be reunited with the primordial Source. Within the reasonable limitations of eternity, there should be more than enough time for each and all to be reunited with The Source. Therefore, rather than being a philosophically pessimistic belief, it was in fact a highly optimistic view in that there is ultimately a happy ending for all. With their belief that 'the body is always innocent,' then should a culprit be required, it would be the mind - so why punish the always innocent body?

The 'two greatest goods' to the anti-materialistic Cathar *Perfecti* were 'gratitude for existence' (not merely this current life) and 'the absolute acceptance of necessity.' Meaning, that one needs to totally accept that all of of this life's experiences as well as that all one's previous lifetime's experiences were necessary to arrive at this very point in time.

Absolute acceptance of this concept allows one to acquire an inner tranquility of soul from an understanding of one's self and one's place within the fabric of the cosmos - though easier said than done.

Added to these basic Cathar beliefs, was their total lack of Judeo/Christian/Islamic devils and demons, guilty fleshy sin and pointless sorrow; damnable hell or fluffy heaven. These theological beliefs starkly contrast with the Cathar's final blissful ending for all through the ultimate reunification of the Divine Spark (which is our unchanging individuality, our unique essence, as distinct from our soul) with the primordial Source from whence it was first created.

'Reunification with The Source' was the Cathar's entire purpose for existence, very different to the worshipping of the loving but vengeful God of the 'Great Faiths.' Truly, this blissful journey's end goal of reunification with The Source, must make Catharism, along with its lack of guilt and deistic punishment, the most stress-free of all major beliefs systems.

Should you be unaware of 'outer guidance' or 'spirit guidance', let me state that these 'dialogues' were not 'channelled', nor are they 'revelations'. They are simply conversations between two human beings, albeit one alive and the other dead; or as Henri put it, "One is encased in the flesh and the other is dis-embodied." The live one, Guillaume de Mirepoix (Jim Callaghan) is questioning his Guide and mentor, Henri de Nebours, who replies in his own inimitable manner.

Mentioned in the book, is Matheus, my Medieval Cathar name, but now Johny Bineham. Though this book is not about me or my Guide. Even so, it was my spirit Guide, Braida de Montserver, who really got things under way, 'got the show on the road', by directing me to make Jim Callaghan (Guillaume) become aware of spirit guidance. These 'Dialogues' actually commenced when Braida mentioned to me that my friend, Guillaume, had been burnt at Montsegur along with her, myself, and 200 others courtesy of the Catholic Church. A religion which never had much truck with heretics who strayed from the loving but rather unforgiving arms of the Holy Mother the Church.

I spoke to Guillaume on various occasions about my personal

experiences with my Guide, Braida. Although quite accepting of my spirit connection, he was somewhat more than surprised when his own Guide, Henri de Nebours, arrived on the scene to make himself known to Jim, who I will now refer to as Guillaume, for that is how Henri always addressed him.

In reference to Outer Guidance, many are unaware that Carl Jung's spirit Guide was named Philemon (Jung referred to him as his Guru). Guides though not rare, are rarely discussed for obvious reasons, the most likely one being that others may consider one a 'nutter'. As well, describing 'outer guidance' to another, is a little like describing childbirth to someone who hasn't experienced it - virtually impossible.

On the question of belief, do I expect you, a 'reasonable person', to accept what is written herein?

I suppose it ultimately depends on where your own life experience, as well as reasoning, has already taken you. Personally, I believe in 'reality over ideology' every time, a necessary adjunct should one think of becoming a Gnostic.

As regards faith, I liked the comment of Bruce Bartlett, a policy adviser to President Ronald Reagan, on describing President Bush, "He truly believes he's on a mission from God. Absolute faith like that overwhelms a need for analysis. The whole thing about faith is to believe things for which there is no empirical evidence." Pause, "But you can't run the world on faith."

Concerning this book, for most neither faith or empirical evidence is of much help. What will matter though, is the depth and resonance you feel vibrating within your inner being while reading the conversations between Henri and Guillaume.

Please don't envision in your mind's eye that that Henri de Nebours wass some meek and mild Cathar cleric. No sir! Henri was built like a Rugby front row forward. This became quite obvious when Henri made his presence visible to Guillaume on three separate occasions.

In *The Cathar Dialogues* Henri makes his salient points bluntly but clearly. Also, he has the happy knack of making clear some areas overly muddied by obtuse philosophical argument. It is worth noting that the Cathar philosophy espoused within the book is not just the musings of one Cathar *Perfecti*. No, this discerning Cathar knowledge was taught to Henri de Nebours by Dion, who he describes as, "The greatest yet most obscure of all the Cathar mystics." Dion's key Catharistic philosophy, as espoused by Henri de Nebours, sets out evolved Cathar beliefs in a manner that is easily understood, as well as holding good at a universal level while highly significant for this and any other age. The primary purpose of *The Cathar Dialogues* is for each, for many, or for all, to take from the discussions that what they may. More important, they are not intended to be used as the basis of some religious belief; the world has more than enough doctrines without the imposition of yet another. However, what *The Cathar Dialogues* herein do contain, is the relevance of Catharistic philosophic thought, which may provide some insights and answers for the reader to assist in lightening life's journey's burdens.

I realise that some may place this book in the genre of the absurd, but I am also buoyed by the belief that it will open the eyes, the mind, and at times, the soul, of those who are ready and waiting for such a book as this.

I hope that you the reader will derive some knowledge, some amusement, as well as some spiritual insights from Henri's informative discussions.

Matheus.
Johny Bineham

Introduction

What you will find exposed in this book is the heart, the mind and the soul of an educated, advanced, Gnostic Cathar perfectus, a Cathar cleric. His discussions ably demonstrate that evolved Gnostic Catharism is universally relevant for this and any future age; albeit, not for the masses.

Gnosticism

True Gnosticism, as remarked by Henri, is so high and remote that it transcends religious beliefs, consequently, it appeals to the solitary traveller rather than those requiring religion. True Gnosticism is an individual internal knowing; it therefore has no necessity for external religious trappings of ritual, temple or dogma. Rather than religious doctrines, true Gnosticism holds that it is sacred knowledge based on one's inner knowing, 'knowledge of the heart,' which is the essential key necessary to unlock the portal to our primary purpose of existence, which is the reunification of our Divine Spark with the primordial Source.

This is ancient knowledge spanning countries, cultures and centuries. This knowledge of the few was invariably persecuted by the multitude. However and thankfully, times have indeed changed, for in this age of information old ideas are made new again; made plain for all to see, to evaluate, to take on board, or to discard.

The advanced Cathar Perfecti of old carried within themselves, bellies full of fire, based on a blissful inner joy derived from knowing 'gnosticly' that they were heading towards a primordial Source, which though essentially unknown, was emanating pure unconditional love for all of creation.

Conversely, the Great Faiths share the common belief of a God's love subject to a conditional final judgement, with a verdict of vengeance for the sinful which includes eternal fiery damnation for a range of variable canonical sins that change complexion, sentence and duration within religion, culture and century.

Contrasting with this Deistic system of reward and reprisal, Catharism could be reduced to a non-judgemental, non-retributive pacifist belief, encompassing respect and love for all living creatures for each is tethered to its Divine Spark. As such, the Cathars were Buddhist-like in holding that all life was sacred and needs be respected. Unlike Buddhists though, both male and female Cathars were held to be spiritually, biologically and intellectually equal. The Cathars also believed that each and all are evolving spiritually over lifetimes. Religion, apparently being one of those necessary stages along most everyone's journey and as such, the religious person, more than their theology, needs to be respected.

To be a Gnostic means that you 'know,' whereas to be an Agnostic means that you 'don't know'. However, what the Gnostic, the Agnostic, the Atheist and the Sceptic have in common, is that they collectively do not kill their fellow human beings for the 'Greater Glory of God,' as has been the practice of Islam and Christianity, over the centuries, even to the present day. Not to be left out entirely, some contemporary Jewish Fundamentalists, like all good Fundamentalists, are also out and about to do God's work. It seems a pity that these people don't feel that their particular deity isn't powerful or strong enough to do his/she/it's work and needs a helping human hand.

I did like though, the answer of the moderate New York Jewish Rabbi visiting Israel, when asked by a Fundamentalist Rabbi, "Don't you believe in God?"

"Yes," he replied, "but it's not the God that you believe in!"

Religion by its very nature, forever resists any changes to its definitive dogmas for each belief has been hewn from the hard stone of its theology over the centuries. Consequently, religion finds itself forever at war with science, empirical knowledge, and just plain common sense.

As Henri put it: "Theologies have never saved people from suffering, pain, anguish and the awful emptiness of life. Actually, they fail to see that this 'emptiness' is the most important indicator in their lives. It is to this 'emptiness' that The Source draws you. This emptiness is the Spark yearning for reunion with The Source. "

Henri's commonsense comment about religion was, "Do not enter into extensive worries about religious forms. Most religions degenerate into moral systems which are designed for social controls. It is better to develop ethical rather than moral systems. Moral systems state, 'you mustn't do this'. A truly ethical system always considers the individual soul in the apportionment of social, legal or personal responsibility."

On the vexed question of sin and sinning (offences against The Source), Henri commented: "The 'offences' against The Source are not subject to some punishment from The Source; they are punished by the soul itself. In fact, it is impossible for the soul to sin against The Source. "

"Whatever denial or activity of body or mind that has a spiritual dimension is either rewarded or punished by the soul itself; sometimes this self-punishment goes on over vast stretches of time. I truly believe that eventually every Spark becomes reunited with The Source."

Spirit Guides

The setting for the opening stages of this book was mundane enough. Two old army mates, Jim Callaghan and John Bineham, both of whom and experienced their fair share of controlled violence during the latter stages of the Korean War. Later, one took a monastic path, while the other volunteered for a few more wars.

One had a literary heart, the other an artistic soul, although I fear, little of merit issued from either. However, what we did have in common was a quest for a pure spirituality; a search for the sacred; unsullied and unshackled by religion.

Later in life, I bumbled onto, rather than discovered my Guide, who happened to be Braida de Montserver, a female Cathar perfecta who was consumed by the flames during the early hours of the morning at Montsegur, on 16th March, 1244, along with over two hundred others including myself and Guillaume.

I had presumed that my Guide, Braida de Montserver, was an old lady, but my daughter, who has a decided psychic streak, said, "No, she is around forty. She is beautiful and looks very similar to Janet Leigh, the movie star, although she has deep set blue eyes."

I queried, "How do you know?"

She said, "I can see her standing there beside you." She went on to describe how she had long blonde hair and wore long dark blue but sometimes dark green gowns.

What I found interesting was that my daughter knew nothing about the Cathars, let alone that they always wore black until persecuted by the Inquisition when they took to wearing both dark blue and dark green coloured clothing.

Early in our friendship, I had many talks with Guillaume about Guides generally, as well as specifically discussing my Guide, Braida. Looking back, I treasured immensely my conversations with Guillaume for he had an enviable intellect powered by a high revving brain which was usually running two steps ahead of the current conversation. This would occasionally cause myself and others varying degrees of annoyance, ranging from mildly vexation to high irritation. Yet, all loved him dearly, for he had the most caring of hearts. I therefore presumed it was his tender heart which came into play for he never challenged me intellectually, or cynically, regarding my relationship with Braida. Actually, we were both unaware then that our present association was the continuation of a friendship that stretched back into ages and lifetimes past.

I and others are indebted for the conscientious work performed by Guillaume, who painstakingly wrote down the conversations with Henri in long hand, then entered them meticulously into the computer using the busy two fingers method. My personal and eternal thanks to you Guillaume.
Matheus
Johny Bineham

CHAPTER I

The journey begins.

March 1999.
I had a session with Braida, my Guide, who told that Guillaume was burnt with me and the two hundred others at Montsegur, in 1244. I mentioned this anecdote to Guillaume who didn't seem particularly surprised.

Thursday, 8th April 1999.
Guillaume seems to acting as a form of conduit. He rang me one morning with messages he jotted down 'for Matheus' on the pad alongside his bed on the night of Friday 26 February 1999. He said it was rare for him to receive more than one message, let alone eight in one evening with specific names, and, for another person. The messages he received for me, "You are the only one I know by that name." were:

1   Let go - cease resisting.
2   Meredith Dolan, good, but caution.
3   Big trees - easy does it.
4   Beware of Cyril, his reality is not your reality.
5   Remember the holy ones given to you.
6   Sapphire-blue, most beautiful transparency
       of joy. In sapphire your needs.
7   The child of both love and honour, that has
       each parent in it.

I could immediately relate to messages 1, 4 and 5. The others

were a complete mystery to me; but they each unveiled themselves over time.

My understanding of the messages:
. 1   Cease resisting my previous Cathar lifetimes.
. 2   Meredith Dolan. I needed to check this out.
. 3   Big trees. My unit is surrounded by big trees - easy does
it ... keep working without pushing.
. 4   Beware of Cyril ... Cyril was a Scientologist.
  5   Remember the holy ones... remember my Guides.
. 6   Sapphire blue ... Merimbula is the Sapphire Coast.
. 7   The child of both love and honour ... My mother was
very loving and my father very honourable.

About two weeks later, Guillaume said he felt that Meridith
Dolan was someone in Merimbula. He had Cyril check on the
Internet if there was any one by that name in Merimbula. Later
Guillaume rang with both the home and business number of an
Meredith Dolan. I said I would ring and check it out next Tues-
day when we meet for lunch.

Tuesday, 13 April 1999.
After Guillaume arrived, I rang Merimbula and a message of an
answer phone stated. 'Meredith Dolan is unavailable at the moment.'

I left a message saying that I intended moving to Merimbula and I would appreciate some information about the area. I
would ring again in a few days time.

Thursday, 15th April 1999.
I went in to see Ralph Nicola, a jeweller friend. Whilst there I
told him the story of M.D. He asked, "When are you going to

ring Merimbula to solve the mystery?"

I gave him the phone number; he rang only to find it engaged. Half an hour later I phoned up Meredith Dolan yet again. This time she answered saying, "I wondered when the mystery phone caller was going to ring back."

She then asked, "How did you get my name?"

"There is nothing like the truth." I replied, "Although, I already feel that you are a spiritual and mystical person."

She said, "I teach Yoga and I am a Reiki Master level 3."

"I thought so. Regarding yourself, a friend of mine who keeps a note pad beside his bed woke up with seven messages for me. One message mentioned your name. My friend Guillaume said he thought it was to do with Merimbula and therefore had a friend check on Internet to see if there was a Meredith Dolan in Merimbula."

"A friend Cyril, found there was and a phone number, but did make the suggestion that Meredith could be either a make or female. In any case, I rang and left a message on your answer phone. In our present conversation, you said you were indeed the person in question."

She said, "I know they work in mysterious ways but this is the strangest yet. So what information do you need?"

I mentioned that I could be looking for a house some time in the future. At present, I just needed to know if there was a caravan park in the town I could stay at?

April 1999.
Sometime during the month, another message flashed for Guillaume, which was:

"The sacred rooms of reason are empty for you now."

Early May 1999.
Guillaume rang to say his book club now had in stock a publica-

tion by the name, *Massacre At Montsegur* by Zoe Oldenbourg.
 I asked him to buy it for me as it has been out of print for some time. He said, "That's where you said we were both burnt, isn't it? No! I'll buy it for myself, later, you can also read it."

CHAPTER II

Henri's first communication with Guillaume.

Thursday, 3rd June 1999.

This morning Guillaume rang somewhat shaken and disturbed. He had woken around five in the morning with the strong premonition that he had to read the transcript of my session with Suzy the medium, which he had in his possession for several days. After he had read the transcript around five in the morning, this voice as clear as a bell, both internal and external, said:

"I am Henry of Nebours, I am your Guide, mentor, and assistant.

I bring you all love, consolation, and important reminders of that reality from which you have so fruitlessly fled. My words to you are not commands. Their strength will be in the resonance they have in your soul but do not lightly reject what I say.

The Spirit is without form or image and in the Spirit you may immerse yourself without fear and in supreme felicity.

This union dispels all fancy and shuts out all forms. It raises the memory to the supernatural and then you will know truth because in these intervals the Spirit works in you.

You have work to do. Consider these questions:

Should I ever smoke again?

Should l ever drink again?

Substantial work is afoot. Substantial work does not mean that it will seen by everyone to be substantial.

You have let Matheus down before. This is your chance to repair all ills that lie between you. Be curious. Discard triviality. Forgive one another. Let there be true balance between you and support his work.

Don't disperse your energies by mending the wrangles of others. Matheus must act soon - let this happen. He will have no needs. You will have no needs of one another except the need for forgiveness.

The time is coming when you will remember together, the breathing of the air, the song of the night bird, the grove and its beauty. In that serene night you will remember the flames that consumes and now will give no pain."

He was quite shaken. He said to me that if someone had asked him if he had ever heard voices? He would think they were mad for asking - but not now - this voice was as clear as you talking to me over the phone.

Wednesday, 16th June 1999.
I saw Suzy the medium, for an hour and a half. I had four questions to ask of Braida. One of her answers advised me 'not to be anxious' about progress as everything is going along at its intended rate.

Thursday, 17th June 1999.
I spoke with Guillaume on the phone who informed me, with some degree of anxiety in his voice, that he had another message from Henri who said not to open the book, *The Massacre At Montsegur*, by Zoe Oldenburg, which the mailman had just delivered. It was sealed in plastic wrapping. Henri said to give the book to me unopened. His very words were:

"I suggest you give the book unopened to Matheus.

Do you think that all answers are in books?

Do you not know truth without outer guidance?

Until you let go, this will be the last demonstration.

Understand that Braida is the sister of Pierre-Roger and Arnald-Roger, both knights of the Mirepoix family.

No book will tell you that you were a liege of Mirepoix, a sentry who fruitlessly betrayed Matheus and Pierre.

You Guillaume betrayed them, were still burnt but the treasure (of Montsegur) survived.

Do you remember your dreams of fire and the screams.

It matters not - beware self pity.

Turn inwards to the Light.

Restore order to your life and write, for this is the path you resisted.

Cooperate with Matheus now, without betrayal."

Later that day, Guillaume and I over coffee, discussed the messages. He said that many years ago he had dreams where he was confined within log walls and being burnt to death.

We finished our coffees, then, as suggested by his Guide, Henri de Nebours, I slit open the plastic wrapping and removed it from the book. After anxiously taking back the book, Guillaume's fingers immediately went to the book's voluminous index to look up 'Mirepoix' which was on page 353. The very first paragraphs he read, stated:

The Seige of Montsegur.

We do not know the number of troops guarding the barbican, but they were probably all slaughtered before their comrades from the fortress had time to come to their aid. Now the Crusaders dominated the entire peak, and could bring troops up to the summit with no fear of any counterattack. The narrow space between fortress and barbican protected the defenders, but did not allow them any room to manoeuvre for offensive action. On this occasion, it seems clear, the defenders of Montsegur were the victims of treachery, or quasi-treachery at the very least. The guides, who must have been heavily bribed by the Crusaders, were beyond any doubt in the confidence of the garrison: otherwise it is impossible to see why the besiegers did not find out about the secret approach months earlier.

It was only from this day forward that the defenders of Montsegur appeared to realise that, short of a miracle, they were doomed. It was after the capture of the eastern barbican that the two heretics Matheus and Peter Bonnet left the fortress, taking with them gold and silver bullion, and a great quantity of money, *pecuniam in-nitam,* the treasure in fact, which must now be safely bestowed elsewhere. Imbert de Salas afterwards revealed, during his interrogation that these two men had a secret understanding with the enemy sentries posted by the last road out still accessible to the besieged garrison. The sentries turned out to be from Camon-sur-l'Hers, in the fief of Mirepoix.

Despite this the evacuation of the treasure was an appallingly risky operation, since the route that had to be followed was far harder and more dangerous than the one by which the Crusaders had come up on the night they stormed the barbican. If the garrison of Montsegur waited till this was the only escape-line available; to them before thinking of removing their treasure to safety, the reason must have been that till then they believed the fortress to be impregnable. The gold and silver-doubtless a very considerable sum - was cached by the two *Perfecti* in the woods on the Sabarthes Mountains, till the day arrived when a safer hiding-place could be found for it.

The siege dragged on. A French attempt to surprise the garrison was beaten off without difficulty. The eastern wall was both short and unusually thick; the battering it was getting from the stone-gun could not make any serious impression on it, let alone knock it down. Bertrand tie La Baccalaria hurriedly setup another machine of his own. The perfectus, Matheus, returned to the fortress towards the end of January, bringing with him two crossbowmen - a meagre reinforcement, but better than nothing. Only very dexterous and intrepid men could have risked the climb up the Porteil chimney; and to return to the fortress at such a moment must have required a boundless devotion to the heretics' cause. This same Matheus then went down a second time to seek reinforcements he came back with one man only and some promises which were never fulfilled, doubtless because of the increased vigilance shown by the troops blockading the mountain.

Yet the garrison still had hope. The men-at-arms smuggled in by Matheus were, according to Imbert tie Salas' testimony, sent by Isarn de Fanjeaux, and brought a message from him to Pierre Roger de Mirepoix: the Count of Toulouse wanted to know if Montsegur could hold out on its own till Easter. The two men asserted that the Count (with the Emperor's help) was levying an army to march on Montsegur and raise the siege. Could Pierre-Roger de Mirepoix have placed any trust in so vague and impracticable a promise? It seems more likely that the statements made by Matheus and the two men-at-arms were intended to raise the garrison's morale. Yet the Count had good reasons for asking the men on Montsegur to hold out as long as possible. Matheus' second venture might well have achieved very tangible results. He had persuaded two local seigneurs, Bernard d'Alion and Arnald d'Usson, to get in touch with a man well capable of saving the situation. This was an Aragonese mercenary captain called Corbario: the two knights promised him fifty livres melgorieries if he would bring twenty five of his men-at-arms to Montsegur. It is clear that these troops belonged to an Aragonese corps d'elite, where each man was versed in all the arts of war, and a match for any knight. With the aid of the garrison these mercenaries would have been quite capable of driving the French back from their advanced position and setting fire to their siege-engine. But Corbario could not break through the lines of the besieging army, which were closer-drawn than ever before. This time Montsegur really was cut off from the outside world with a vengeance, and could no longer rely on any external assistance.

The fortress held out all through February. William de Puy-laurens says that 'no rest was given to the besieged, either by day or night.' The stone-gun kept up a constant barrage, making it impossible to erect any defensive fortifications on the wall under fire. Inside the fortress shortage of space was making life quite unbearable: hundreds of people were literally jostling against one another.

From all this I now know that I was Matheus, the *perfectus*. Braida (my present spirit Guide) was the sister of Arnold and Pierre Roger de Mirepoix, who was Montsegur's garrison commander. Braida, Guillaume and I, Matheus, were burnt on that same day along with the two hundred other heretics who refused to recant.

It also tells us that whatever the 'treasure' consisted of, it was carried down the cliffs by heretics Matheus and Pierre Bonnet. Obviously, the treasure may have been heavy but not so weighty that it would prevent two strong men from carrying it down the vertical porteil. As well, it must have been sufficiently precious and/or sacred, that it remained with the Cathars on the mountain top until virtually the last days of the siege.

June 1999.
Transcript of a tape recording I made with Guillaume.

After having coffee with Guillaume, I brought out my tape recorder, switched it to record as I wanted Guillaume to explain in his own words what it felt like on the first occasion that Henri de Nebours spoke to him.

G: "Would you like me to tell you? I'll tell you straight forward.

29

M: Yes, that would be a change!

G: Yes! Anyway I went to bed on the night of 2nd of June, 1999, and towards morning on the 3rd, I had a dream which I have had before many times, I am down in the basement or a crypt, or whatever, and there is an old man talking in front of a lectern or behind a curtain, it's always been a recurring dream, I've never understood what he said but on this occasion I heard it quite distinctly. I had a transcript of your session with Suzy, I've been intending to read it but hadn't because I found it rather boring. Ha! Ha! But he said quite clearly, "You should read it." I can't remember exactly what he said but that was the purport of it. So I got up, I had to get up and have a pee anyway. I got up and started to read it. So when I read it I put down and thought about it for a few minutes.

M: It wouldn't take many more than that!

G: M-m-m, then I heard a voice; it makes me sound as if there was a loud speaker outside but it wasn't like that. I'll talk about that in a minute; what the voice was like...

M.   It sounded clear anyway.

G.   It was quite clear. I always buy pads by the dozen - writing pads. I've always got them around the house to write things down and I picked it up and wrote what I heard. I've given you the text, and it had a powerful emotional effect on me, I don't know why, I mean, I was a bit surprised by it all. Surprise is not the right word.

M.   Taken aback!

G.   I was disturbed by it. Well, it was an unusual experience. I've always acquainted hearing voices with schizophrenia, but that's not like how the voice was. It was both external and internal at the same time, if that makes sense to you. I had a sense - the style is more different from my own

M.   More lyrical?

G.   More lyrical - yes, and it's freer.

M   I notice they invariably use small words, not multi-syllable words.

G.   I didn't notice that but there are some lovely phrases in it, like, a reference to 'a serene grove.'

M.   That's right.

G.   It's a lovely phrase - a serene grove. Things like that, the choice of words were different - and basically that was it. I wrote it out and later on, that morning, I wrote a copy for you. No, it was actually that might, 7.30 that night. I was feeling really tired so I laid down as I had to ring someone at 10.30.

M.   That night was no different to any other?

G.   No. I hadn't been smoking any strange substances or injecting myself with anything, or taking any pills, except the pills I've been taking for years. No! I wasn't pissed, or sad, or particularly ecstatic, I felt quite well, I went to bed at half past ten.

M.   In all respects it was a normal night,

G.   It was, yeh - but the emotional impact was what shook me a bit. Also I'm a great one for wanting to think things through, looking for an obvious explanation. Was it a a spirit communication?

 The voice said, "I am Henri of Nebours." I checked out the name of the town in a couple of French books I've been reading lately that had French towns in it; I checked the indexes but I couldn't find that town anywhere. So whether such a town existed or not, I don't know but my mind works that way; I tend to think of explanations and this is a subject I've been discussing with you for some time.

M.   Rational explanations.

G.   But it did disturb me because I've often - all my life I've written things when I woke up in the morning, sort of fragments of dreams, things that have hovered around in my head and so on. Sometimes its been the inspiration for a poem or poems. Sometimes they had a particularly elegant form of words. I don't know why this is, but some little while ago, it must be some months ago, I'd written down a very clear recollection of a dream.

M.   That's right - eight messages.

G.   Tell Matheus to contact Meredith Dolan in Merimbula. A very specific message.

M.   Well, we didn't know it was Merimbula at the time.

G.   Did I write a copy for you?

M.   No, we found out from Cyril on the Internet But there was an Meredith Dolan in Merimbula.

G.   Well my thought was, where did such a specific name come from? It's not - so I try to hunt around in my mind if I ever knew of an Meredith Dolan, even if I've seen it in the phone book, I wouldn't have known whether it was Meredith Dolan or whatever. Why do you want me to read this? This is the text of what I wrote down.

M.   For the fact that it is your handwriting and you're reading it. Well, you can read your handwriting much better than I can.

G.   OK.   You are not going to advertise this, or put it on the Internet. You know, I don't want people to think that I'm a ratbag. The message, the script that I wrote, said:

"I am Henry of Nebours, I am your Guide, mentor, and assistant.

I bring you all love, consolation, and important reminders of that reality from which you have so fruitlessly fled. My words to you are not commands. Their strength will be in the resonance they have in your soul but do not lightly reject what I say.

The Spirit is without form or image and in the Spirit you may immerse yourself without fear and in supreme felicity.

This union dispels all fancy and shuts out all forms. It raises the memory to the supernatural and then you will know truth because in these intervals the Spirit works in you.

You have work to do. Consider these questions:

Should I ever smoke again?

Should I ever drink again?

Substantial work is afoot. Substantial work does not mean that it will seen by everyone to be substantial.

You have let Matheus down before. This is your chance to repair all ills that lie between you. Be curious. Discard triviality. Forgive one another. Let there be true balance between you and support his work.

Don't disperse your energies by mending the wrangles of others. Matheus must act soon - let this happen. He will have no needs. You will have no needs of one another except the need for forgiveness.

The time is coming when you will remember together, the breathing of the air, the song of the night bird, the grove and its beauty. In that serene night you will remember the flames that consumes and now will give no pain.

G.   That's the end of it."

Thursday 17 June 1999.

I also asked Guillaume to read aloud his second message from Henri so I could tape it. This was on the same day he gave the transcript to me.

M.   "Whenever you're ready. Thursday 17th ... I'll just read out what I wrote you this morning:

'I suggest you give the book unopened to Matheus.

Do you think that all answers are in books?

Do you not know truth without outer guidance?

Until you let go, this will be the last demonstration.

Understand that Braida - Braida, I've written - is the sister of Pierre-Roger - I've written Pierre and Roget - and Arnald-Roger - I've spelt that, Arnold and Roget, both knights of the Mirepoix family - I've spelt that Meurpois .

No book will tell you that you were a liege of Mirepoix, a sentry who fruitlessly betrayed Matheus - I've spelt that Mathios, because the that's the way I heard it - and Pierre.

You Guillaume betrayed them, were still burnt but the treasure survived.

Do you remember your dreams of fire and the screams.

It matters not - beware self pity.

Turn inwards to the Light.

Restore order to your life and write, for this is the path you resisted.

Cooperate with Matheus now, without betrayal.' And that's the whole box and dice"

Listening to these tapes fills me with nostalgia and regret. I wish now, I had recorded many more of our conversations. Listening to these tapes; listening to his deep distinctive melodic voice, reminds me of how much I miss his company.

I'm sure one the pleasures of departure from this mortal plane will be rejoining all those you miss terribly who have died before you. I certainly miss your company, Guillaume.

Thursday, 24th June 1999.

Suzy, the medium, rang this morning to cancel the appointment. I will ring for another.

Guillaume also rang to say he had an incredible experience. He had a visitation by Henri and two Cathar women, which has already made big changes for him. He said that one effect was an infusion of knowledge. As well, he now fervently believes in reincarnation which he couldn't rationalise before this occurrence. He also believed he was now clairvoyant, and importantly, his sight had improved.

What actually transpired was that Guillaume actually saw Henri which gave him quite a fright for he saw him quite plainly. He was told by Henri to lay down and place a pillow under both his head and ankles. Guillaume closed his eyes but was told to open them so he could see and record what was occurring.

Henri proceeded to extract the pips from twelve fresh olives. A cloth was placed in a pestle with the olives wrapped inside. They were then mashed thoroughly with the pestle. The cloth was then squeezed until a small portion of olive oil was extracted.

Henri continued to anoint Guillaume's head, rubbing in the oil vigourously with the side of his palm. At the same time, two Cathar women rubbed and kneaded some of the olive oil into the soles of his bare feet. One used her knuckles; the other used the heel of her palm. After some time they swapped places, continuing with the massage. The whole process took about three hours. Henri said that it was one of the secret Cathar rituals and that I would also be experiencing the same procedure.

Henri did comment that he, Guillaume, was a thinker and a writer, while I was a healer and a man of action. I suppose that I am conscious of such and am now champing at the bit to be up and doing that which I was born for.

July 1999.

Braida told me to inform Guillaume that in a previous lifetime, both he and I were Cathars who together were burnt to death on the same occasion.

When I next met Guillaume, I suggested he ask Henri how many times he was burnt to death?

A few days later he rang to say that Henri informed him that he was burnt to death on three occasions. The first was by the sun, ending an Egyptian lifetime. The second was at Montsegur, but what Matheus's Guide Braida, was referring to, was in a later lifetime when, we were yet again burnt together by the Inquisition at Firenza in Italy. (Interestingly, as a child I used to tell my friends that I didn't care how I actually died just so long as I wasn't burnt to death).

CHAPTER III

The First Dialogue

Thursday, 12th August 1999.

Guillaume had another session with his Guide, Henri of Nebours. Guillaume rang me about it on the following day. Guillaume was having some misgivings and doubts about what was occurring. He asked Henri the following questions:

G: "I am filled about doubts about the future?

H: Children use the loom of darkness to weave fantasies of fear. Do not use your ignorance of the future to knit pointless anxiety into the cloak of paralysis.

G: Do you know the future? Can you tell me about it?

H: The future is unknown in concrete terms, but if you use your skilled tongue and adroit mind to turn a scorpion into a rose today, do not be astounded if a rose fatally stings you tomorrow. You and I and all of us, in God, write the future by what we do and say and think today. We write our own future realities.

G: Are you my leader? If so tell me what to do.

H: Discard ideas of leadership. Waiting for leadership is waiting for emptiness. I am you guide and mentor, I do not lead you. You are totally free. Be led by love. Be led by the reality now presenting itself.

G: Why can't I stop smoking?

H: What will satisfy you? Ask yourself these questions: Have I received the highest gifts? Have my eyes been opened? My ears unblocked? I will tell you a nursery story.

'Once upon a time a dog was captured by an evil man and tied to a post by an iron chain. Round and round the dog walked until no blade of grass grew within the reaches of the chain. Still the dog walked round and round, hungry, dirty, and tired within the circle of the chain for year after year.

One day his master called. The dog barked and became frantic but could not leave the circle he had trodden. 'You stupid dog,' his master said, 'the chain rusted away long ago, come!'

Guillaume do not love your broken chains.

G: Is Matheus my leader?

H: Two men walk together in a forest. One walks in front for a time with the map, at another time his companion walks in front with the compass. Which of those two men are the leader? Or are both led by their goal? When the map is needed, so be it. When the compass is needed, let it be so, but always press onward to the goal. Always consider the ends and the means will come to hand.

G: I feel ashamed to talk to you about some things. I have worried about 'Meridith Dolan' and Merimbula. The night Matheus went he had no money. He didn't see Meridith Dolan; I felt afterwards it was because he could not invite her to dinner. In short I'm saying that money is important. What is the significance of Meridith Dolan? What about money? I'm really sorry to be so confused about this stuff. Please tell me what you can.

H: Be calm Guillaume. Let me tell you what you already know, it is this: 'Hold not too tightly nor too lightly.' Be anxious about nothing. Stop now for awhile and go to your 'inner room' and I will speak to you again shortly."

Later on that evening:

H: "My mention of Meredith Dolan was to break through to you with a clear and irrefutable demonstration. You have known me for a long time, but though you know me and yet you would not know me.

This helped you to open your inner door to me. As to money, I do know what you know, I do not and cannot pour physical money into your lap but I will give you a demonstration very soon, it will be in this wise, If you were in the desert and you asked for water, my first recourse would be to influence someone to come to your aid; failing this I would revive in your memory how water is found in deserts.

Other means would be tried in progression after this. In other words the first step is through man. You taught me that, 'Merit moves from man to man and not from man, 0 Lord, to thee.' Remember?'

So in a very short time I will arrange for money to come to you, not for any purpose as you suppose, but as a demonstration. This money will come to you with puzzling and ambiguous conditions attached, this will make it clear that I am the source.

Do not let your faith be based on demonstration however, but rather the calm certainty of a crop which lies in the bosom of the planting farmer.

Do not hesitate to call on me at any time. We are tied by ancient bonds.

Farewell Guillaume, wait and pray with this thought in mind: *When the goal is clear and your will is fixed, then energy is created. Energy creates the means.*"

Thursday, 19th August 1999.

Guillaume had a running nose for about three weeks; it was getting steadily worse. He rang me for help. He said it was dripping continuously to the point that it was embarrassing. I said I would write a Chinese herbal script for him.

By the time we had finished talking about half and hour later the drip had stopped. I rang the following Sunday to say I had written out a script (I was a trained Chinese Herbalist so I wrote my scripts in Chinese characters, 'Hanzi'), however, he said it hasn't reoccurred since it stopped dripping soon after he rang me on Thursday night.

Thursday, 21st October 1999.

Guillaume by now had developed quite a working relationship with Henri. Guillaume related to me some of the comments Henri had made, such as:

H: "What we believe is the truth for now. Don't be trapped by beliefs!

Regards the future-it is the journey rather than the destination. Future events are even now casting its shadow. Major events are about to happen!"

G: Is it to do with Matheus?

H: Probably!"

CHAPTER IV

The Second Dialogue.

July 2000.

G: "I have always been interested in the big questions; that is the sort of thing I'd like to talk with you about.

H: Epicurus once said: *'Just as medicine confers no benefit if it does not drive away physical illness, so philosophy is useless if it does not drive away the suffering of the mind'.*

Ask yourself why are you interested in the big questions; if you knew how the stars were formed would you be happier? If all knowledge of the 'big questions' were opened to you - what then? Perhaps we might look at an example of one of these questions.

G: Well, for instance; 'If God is all good, why is there so much suffering in the world?'

H: How well formulated this oft-asked question is and how meaningless. How much suffering is there in the world? Are there great oceans of it; are there enormous mountains of it (if you prefer a terrestrial rather than an aqueous metaphor)?

You would answer me with the examples of six million Jews tortured: you run through your mind, memories of suffering you have seen in war; memories of horrors in Rwanda; recounting of the desperate injustices in Palestine or Sri Lanka. If you were to go back in time and space there are almost countless chilling and compelling examples you could give me in your indictment (or questioning) of the 'Goodness of God.' How meaningless this all is; I could play semantic and here and ask you to define 'goodness' and 'God,' and ask you in what sense the preposition 'of' can be invoked to link God with the possession of your concept of 'goodness,' but I said from the start that I was not interested in discussing with you 'philosophical ideas.'

We men have an incredible capacity to reify abstractions. The suffering of one man is not an abstraction. The suffering of six million men is an abstraction; it has no reality: let me explain. If one man, Joseph, is tortured and killed, his suffering is real. Let us imagine that he has borne the maximum pain that a human body is capable of bearing consciously. If another man, Benjamin, is now subjected to the same treatment, does the 'amount' of suffering double? Of course not. Why weep over the suffering of the millions of gazelles eaten over the centuries by lions, tigers, hyenas and crocodiles? Why weep over the suffering of six million men? Should we not rather look to the suffering we see around us and, in this individual pain, see the appropriate object for our sympathy, empathy and assistance rather than spending our time moaning over 'the suffering of millions.'

G: But the problem of pain has been a major theological and philosophical question since the beginning of recorded history and probably for millennia before that.

H: I'm sure you're right, but it is an individual problem rather than a cumulative or community problem. I must explain this; when Vesuvius erupts and thousands suffer and die, each individual suffers and/or dies. This certainly poses community problems; how to clear away so many dead, how to alleviate the sufferings of each individual how to house each survivor. I must reiterate that the pain and suffering are not cumulative. It is our capacity for making a single thing out of a collection of things that makes it seem so. We are constantly falling into error in our thinking by making abstractions into (apparently) real things.

I invite you to observe, in history and your experience, how frequently the greatest harm is done by individuals who profess a large, generalised capacity for compassion. This professional compassion for mankind at large seldom finds a focus in any individual.

In fact, think of the suffering caused by 'compassionate philosophies': communism is, in its roots and expressions is a deeply 'compassionate philosophy'; so is Christianity; so is Hinduism and many other 'big ideas.' If this is so, then why the Gulags, why the Crusades, why the caste system? Why the rejection of the fruits of reason (science)? The answer is, those who focus on the 'big questions' neglect, very often, the individual who is suffering under the 'big questioner's' very nose.

G: I know what you're saying is true but many good men have thought of great schemes for alleviating the lot of their fellowman only to find their ideas perverted after their death, or even in their lifetime, by their followers - St Francis of Assisi for instance.

H: What you say has some truth, but you may be overestimating the goodness of the idea, and perhaps the virtue of the man conceiving the idea. May I suggest to you, that you Guillaume, have an unfortunate propensity to think well of others whilst, simultaneously, thinking the worst of yourself?

You have often in the past had hero-worship for great thinkers or 'saints' or good people isn't that so? Isn't it true that your training has, on the other hand, given you an almost morbid level of self-criticism? This is not entirely bad, but it has locked you into a very cautious degree of self-assessment of your own ideas ... couple this with your inclination to acceptance of the conventional, as you have done, and one is describing a pathological condition; you have been saved the pathology, but only because you have a reasonable level of common sense. But you must discard the trust in authority which characterises your nature: relax, let go.

There are many thrones in the world: there have been many thrones in the past; thrones of Roman Emperors; thrones of Popes; thrones of Holy Roman Emperors; thrones of autocratic Tsars ... remember what I am about to say and apply it in the widest sense to kings, generals, philosophers, popes, cardinals, professors and even to yourself:

The man who sits on the highest throne is still sitting on an arse!

G: You certainly have a pithy mode of expression.

H: Better than a prissy search for euphemisms.

G: I was talking before about Francis of Assisi ... now there was a good man, surely.

H: He was a man, that is enough to say about him, in itself. As to the quality of goodness ... I am not so ready to assign or deny this attribute to any man. You seem, Guillaume, to want these models of Perfection. Don't do it, all you achieve is to make yourself feel inadequate and less than others. You know this is an absurdity.

G: That may be true, but what of Francis? Surely if ever there was a good man he was one.

H: If you insist; Francis tried to get the Pope to authorise him to lead a crusade to liberate Jerusalem. Perhaps he knew nothing of the history of the Crusades, if not then your idea of goodness is not mine; the best we can say about this ill-advised career move is that it was founded on ignorance. Then he founded (with the Pope's permission) the Mendicant Order of Friars Minor; they would own nothing, no houses, no money, nothing beyond the needs of that day. So the method of subsistence is conveyed in that little word 'mendicant'!

They would live by begging, door-to-door, from the desperately poor and ignorant serfs. This they did in the name of God and not by offering to help their putative donors by doing some work in return for the food. In addition he induced a girl who loved him, Clare, to set up a similar Order for women; including the usual vows of celibacy. Very appropriately they have come to be known as the Poor Clares. Further, Francis was an ecstatic whose soul underwent a mystical marriage with Christ; I won't comment on this beyond saying what a good subject for deep psycho-sexual analysis.

G: You're painting a horrible picture of one of my heroes

H: You did insist, but it is no part of my purpose to denigrate anyone, past or present.

G: Still, a lot of good came out of Francis' life. I think most people would acknowledge that.

H: I can tell that you are becoming irritated by what you consider to be my iconoclasm; but you keep insisting on a point which, to me, is no point. Your assertion that, 'a lot of good came out of Francis' life' is a very interesting one. I know you can make a case for the hospitals, orphanages and hospices inspired by his life but let me put the other side for balance. Let me speak to you a little about a historical incident in which the Franciscans were heavily involved, namely the 'conquest' of what we now call South America.

There are many accounts contemporaneous (or nearly so) with this period. One I would recommend to you is in French, *Tyrannies et cruautes Des Espagnols perpetrees es Indies occidentales qu'on dit le Nouveau Monde,* translated from the Spanish in the late 1570s. The work from which it is translated is by Bartolomeo Las Casas in Spanish but with a different title; Las Casas wrote it in the early 1550s. It tells a horrifying tale of the dreadful destruction of the native populations of Mexico and Peru. By 1530, thirty-eight years after the arrival of Columbus, the empires of the Incas and the Aztecs were completely destroyed and the native peoples were in slavery - except for the recalcitrant, who were summarily murdered. For a variety of reasons (not least of which was their natural hospitality) these people had allowed the Spanish the freedom of their cities and villages. They had no answer to the Spanish response to this generosity. This response was treachery and slaughter on a scale that is extraordinary by any measure.

If you want to talk of mountains of pain and oceans of tears you have it in this story. The fear of the 'Indians' was tremendous, partly because they were given good reason to fear and partly because the level of treachery and mindless violence was beyond even their experience (and the Aztecs, at least, had customs of human sacrifice).

One incident related by Las Casas may interest you: an Indian woman saw the Conquistadores approaching and she hanged herself with her young child. A soldier cut the child in half and fed his dogs with one half and asked the Franciscan friar accompanying the army to give Extreme Unction to the other half, so the baby would be certain of a place in Heaven. I could go on, but suffice it to say that by 1590 the population of the *Nouveau Monde* had fallen from about 80 million to 10 million: this by best estimate. The book I've suggested may not be immediately available to you, so I'll see what is convenient to fall into your hands.

G: I think Francis would have been horrified at this, as you and I are.

H: What makes you think I'm horrified? As for Francis, don't be so sure; mind you, read back and notice that you have urged me on here, and I'm not attempting to deride or condemn anybody - I do urge you however to consider what he sat upon. This is a fundamental point (excuse the word play). The other point is ... how much good needs to flow, how many hospitals built and staffed, how many orphanages founded and run with love and care, in order to balance this 'mountain of pain and ocean of tears'? The good intentions proverbially providing the paving stones for the Luciferian highway are, I'm sure, generalised good intentions.

G: Surely we can't blame the Franciscans for the excesses of the Spanish conquests?

H: The Spanish con Conquistadores were accompanied by the Franciscans and some proportion of these actively encouraged vile measures; some actively opposed the villainy; but you may be sure that the majority just fitted in with the prevailing ethos ... condonation by silence.

G: The friars would have thought they were bringing the greatest gift possible to the natives, the Christian faith.

45

H: Alas! How often man has attempted to bring 'the greatest good' to others by slaughtering them. The two greatest 'goods' (I'm indulging you with the philosophical jargon) are existence and the absolute acceptance of necessity.

G: I am exhausted, I'll think about what you've told me and speak to you again if I may, after I've absorbed your ideas.

H: I'm always at your disposal, Guillaume, and by all means think. 'Think' does not mean worry. I repeat what I have told you in previous colloquiae ... don't let me steamroller you, you are a free agent and I am only a facilitator, a guide and companion. Sleep well and be gentle with yourself."

2000

Date not noted.

One day over lunch, Guillaume passed on some information concerning me from a conversation that he had with Henri. Henri told Guillaume that when I, Matheus, had tried to teach him Numerology which Henri said was ancient knowledge, but he Guillaume had resisted. So as an exercise he asked Guillaume to give him any two dates of birth. Guillaume gave Henri mine and that of his friend, Dieter.

I have no idea what Henri said about Dieter, but I remember clearly what Henri said about myself, "Because of the influence of a recalcitrant seven in my date of birth, everything that I had attempted in life must end in failure."

Immediately, on hearing this from Guillaume, I felt more of a feeling of relief rather than surprise, because I was more than aware that everything in my life until now had ended in failure. Everything, meaning relationships, businesses and aspirations; everything for one reason or another, had gone belly up. Not-

withstanding this, I was far from being disheartened. On balance, I had outlasted three wars, surviving death on some eight-
een occasions, so I actually considered myself as being a very
lucky person. Though I must confess that this newly acquired
numerological knowledge, courtesy of Henri de Nebours, actually took a great weight off my shoulders; not to mention release
mystification from my mind.

CHAPTER V

The Third Dialogue.

July - September 2000.

G: "Welcome, Henri, I'm sorry to have been so combative in our last session. I am grateful for all the time and effort you spend on my behalf.

H: Guillaume, Guillaume, always so humble and regretful; it's not obligatory to denigrate yourself every time we speak. Do you think I don't get a great measure of delight out of our converse? I have found your thoughts most absorbing for decades now: thank goodness that the breakthrough came and we can have these dialogues. I don't want you just to be a sponge, you have a good mind and I'm often entertained by your insights; let us look on one another as loving friends who enjoy one another's company. What would you like to chat about?

G: I'm not sure, I've been somewhat disturbed by our last conversation. I don't know what's wrong with me.

H: There is nothing wrong. You are feeling disloyal and confused. You accept some of the things I say, but you can't help looking regretfully behind you at discarded mental habits. Do you think that is so?

G: I think you are right but I don't know how to change.

H: Perhaps you look too much at things as if they were challenges; maybe you should accept some things as just things-in-themselves: that's just the way they are.

G: This habit of questioning and seeking is very difficult to break, so too is the habit of self-criticism. When one has spent many years doing a daily examination of conscience the habit becomes very strong.

H: Don't reject anything of your past, remember that you are what you are today because of the many experiences you have lived through: Accept this, learn from it and regret nothing,

G: It is difficult to reject habits of humility (perhaps its self-denigration), meekness, consideration and so on which seem so much the hallmark of Christian thought.

H: Please spare me! I think we should openly discuss some of these things ... if you would like to do so.

G: I don't mind, I'd be very interested to hear your thoughts on these matters.

H: Some of the virtues you talk about are very easy to simulate and very easy to deceive oneself about. So much so that Rae Heap has become a symbol of this bogus humility. True humility is to know the truth about oneself and one's part in the scheme of things ... and most importantly to accept this. As I said before, one of the two greatest gifts is the absolute acceptance of necessity.

G: Changing the subject ... I found a book today, on sale at the library for $2.00. Thank you, Henri. You said you would find out what was convenient to fall into my hands. You know about it, I'm sure but I'll record the details here. The book is called *Memory of Fire* by Eduardo Galeano translated by Cedric Belfrage. I've put the details into my LITERARY folder. Its the first book of a trilogy. Now, did you know that Las Casas was the first priest ordained in the New World? The book is not really 'by' Eduardo Galeano, it is a compilation of quotes from 227 authors and about 280 - 300 books. There are three books quoted by Las Casas: *Brevissima Relacion de la Destruccion de las Indies, Historia de las Indies, Mexico City*: FCE, 1951, *Apologetica historia de las Indies, Mexico City*: LINAM,1 967. There is an interesting quote from Las Casas about a chief called Hatuey, who had fled from the conquerors (A.D.1511):

49

'They catch him three months later. They tie him to a stake before lighting the fire that will reduce him to charcoal and ash. The priest promises him glory and eternal rest if he agrees to be baptised. Hatuey asks: "Are there Christians in that heaven? "Yes!"
Hatuey chooses Hell, and the firewood begins to crackle'.

I know Matheus will be interested in the book. It is a very curious book; I'll discuss it with you when I have studied it. Another strange thing happened today; I bought a book for Dieter's 50th birthday *Consolations of Philosophy* by Alain de Bolton and, as usual, I looked up the index and bibliography and the book you mentioned by Las Casas is quoted in Consolations... as having been read by Montaigne. In fact, this book looks so interesting that I might get a copy of it for myself and read it.

H: I'm delighted that you found the book and these other little coincidences followed. This has happened a lot in the last eight or nine months, Hasn't it?

G: Thanks to you, Henri.

H: Only in part, Guillaume: don't forget that we are all subject to the underlying influences I spoke to you about before. It is only a conjunction of these influences that brought you into conscious contact with me. Also, you have never experienced the same negative flows that Matheus has borne for years.

G: I always knew that I was somehow protected; sometimes this was in quite remarkable ways. I attributed this to my Guardian Angel - often with a wry backward look to my childhood.

H: The important point here was that you did accept that there was a benign entity looking after you. But don't forget either that a wonderful spirit of prayer has suffused your life. Even though this has been misguided many times, nevertheless your disposition has been constant and right. It is better to pray than not to pray.

G: It depends, surely, to whom and to what we pray and,

also, what we pray for. This is something I've discussed often with Matheus; he says that a lot of prayer is only 'transcendental begging'. I agree with him and for years I've tried to avoid that Catholic 'Vale of Tears' and 'wretched sinner' thing.

H: This is an interesting question. Matheus is partly right. The question is really related to the nature of the Great Mystery which we call God. Don't forget that our conversations have the nature of prayer, and when you tell me your concerns I try to do something about them.

G: For which I'm very grateful.

H: The point is that you and I are both instruments of God. As human souls it is fitting that we should do what we can for one another within the limits of the flows occurring in our lives from underlying influences: from the universe, from the realities of any situation and in our minds and souls.

G: I think I follow the general idea, but maybe you could give me a concrete example?

H: An example of an underlying influence from the universe is the frustration built into the life flow of Matheus. This has led to frequent frustration of many of his hopes and plans. He has suffered more pain and stress from this, especially in his younger days, than you can begin to understand: it has demanded from him the exercise of considerable courage, probably greater than a lot of people could tolerate without becoming embittered and sour with life. You know him well enough to know that he is not bitter or sour, rather the reverse.

G: That's true, I often wished I could be more like him.

H: Natural enough, but resist the temptation to any sort of hero-worship. Back to my comments on the underlying influences; we have looked at one concrete example of the underlying 'flow' coming from the universe, now we'll look at examples of the influence of the reality of a given situation. You remember we had a discussion about your worries when B was coming last year? They were mainly financial. Now I'm not in the business of printing bank-notes, but I did see influences working in M and you after you had that serendipitous meeting in the supermarket; I reminded him several times of you (easier because of your recent meeting) until he rang you, and the rest you know.

Similarly, when you discussed with me your concerns about Matheus's finances for his trip to Korea; I told you not to worry and, as you saw, the $600 came to you from a human source, through my prompting. There is not a great deal of mystery about all this, I'll explain some of the 'underlying flows' in regard to supply (money and other needs) for you. You don't know it, but many people are conscious of your worth to them and have planned, at some time or another, to 'reward' you: your poor niece, M, is an example.

G: She's always pestering me about giving me money, or wanting to buy things for me.

H: You know about her because she is so disturbed that she tends to say whatever comes into her mind; but there are others who think this way but, as is the way of we humans, the thought passes. All I have done is reinforce these thoughts. Part of the 'reality of the situation' is the sort of person you are and are perceived to be. People's perception of Matheus is such that his courage and drive make people feel that he has no need of them. This tends to block flows to him of a material nature.

G: I don't have that perception of him.

H: I know, but that has two sources: he has been very open with you, (more than with most men) and you have been able to discuss him with me. We have shared insights.

The last of the 'flows' I mentioned are the 'flows in our own minds and souls.' This is a deep subject but I'll give you a comparison that you will readily see.

I'm going to speak metaphorically; when you encounter an idea or fact that interests you, you tend to 'over-digest' it; when Matheus has the same experience he tends to 'under-digest' it. Look at how many years you spent (wasted?) 'over-digesting' the ideas of ontology and epistemology. Matheus processes ideas in a completely different way, don't you agree?

G: Yes, I find this irritating sometimes.

H: This is because the fundamental 'flows' of your minds and souls is so different; it is really the difference between the man of action and the contemplative man. It is interesting, surely, that Matheus has the soul of an artist and a man of intense activity, whilst you have the soul of a poet, a contemplative and a *literatus* (I'm not commenting on how good at these things either of you are). Two more different 'flows' would be hard to imagine. If it is necessity to build a wall then Matheus is the man (and most probably it would be a beautiful wall); but if it is necessary to build a wall of words then you are the man. Fighting too strongly against these fundamentals makes folly of your lives.

G: I can only agree, in general, with what you said, but I can't help feeling that other unseen forces are at work in our lives, minds and souls.

H: You're right, of course, and one of these forces is very much misunderstood by embodied souls. This is the force of intention; or as you would call it, will.

G: Do you mean 'will' in the sense of 'willpower' or in the scholastic sense?

H: Neither really, fits the bill of what I am talking about here. Willpower, in the Victorian tradition of Matthew Arnold et al. is precisely what I am not talking about; will in the scholastic sense is closer to it, but is still off the mark. That's why I used the word 'intention' before I used the word 'will.'

Intention is the disposition of a mind and a soul towards a real object. The disposition is not one of teeth-gritting determination but rather a complete orientation of the soul towards that object.

G: I understand your point but could you give me an example or two, please?

H: Sometimes you carry your disingenuous act too far with me; I know it amuses you, sometimes, with others, but don't try it on with me!

G: O.K. point taken.

H: Good, that's a better answer than your habitual (and bogus) grovel. We'll get somewhere quicker if we cooperate and you try not to be so defensive. 'Intention' must be formed as completely as possible and all human avenues to its accomplishment thought through to finality. You did this in regard to the money for Matheus. You formed the intention to get it for him and then you thought of a number of ways of raising the money; then, at my prompting, you let go of all these mental machinations and waited.

There is a point in this period of waiting; it is here that, at the deepest level, the intention (the gentle and constant disposition of the will, if you like) comes into accord with the influences working on your life. Now, it may be that one of the plans or ideas you had for raising the money is adopted by you, generally, not so. A seemingly unrelated ('unrelated' in the sense that you don't perceive it as being related to the intention which you fixed on, nor the plans associated with it).

For example, just before you left Toukley you rang your old friend J.M. You knew his circumstances: So he had not figured in your plans for raising money; but he produced the $600 and insisted that you take it in part settlement of the debt you had long forgotten and written off. This was partly my doing, it was certainly his wish; it accorded well with R's gratitude to you for saving the house for the family; it happened, too, that he has improved his position considerably since you had last spoken with him. All these, and other influences, came together under the steady beam of your unwavering but not rigid intention

It was not my assistance, it was not just J.M.'s basic honesty about a commercial debt, nor any other single factor; your intention was fixed, but not rigid (not teeth-gritting). Because of the sort of person you are, many more ways were open to you for raising the money than you had thought of. You have sown prolifically in your life, so it should not amaze you if a time comes when you can reap.

G: So 'intention' is the unwavering but relaxed focussing of the will on an object?

H: Yes, but don't forget my stricture that the object must be real. It is no good bringing intentionality to bear on an object such as 'to raise a lot of money for the good of mankind.' 'The good of mankind' is one of those abstractions to which you are much given, and which I've warned you about.

G: I do understand your point. Is there any part of your instruction which needs emphasis, apart from the stricture on 'reality'?

H: I'm wondering if you have grasped the meaning I have given to the word 'intention.' By this I don't mean that Catholic thing embodied in the word. 'Attention' might be a better word.

The steps are as follows; I'll do this in a form that is deferential to your taste for the tabular presentation of ideas:

*   Form the intention.

*   Focus your attention on it very specifically (visually if that helps).

*   Consider diligently all the ways you can think of to achieve the object.

*   Relax and let go, without abandoning the intention,

Accept that the influences we have discussed are working unseen by you on your intention (these influences are many; some are within you, some are external), certainly use discussion with me or other appropriate persons.

Most importantly, as I've explained to you before, 'expect a miracle.'

If at any time in this process there is a sort of mental 'gripping' or 'teeth-gritting' going on, then back off and let go. Return to your intention at least once daily without exhausting yourself or worrying. The essence of this technique should be well known to you, even though you have never had it formalised like this before.

G: One thing you have not mentioned is, the object should be a good one. This is a technique that can't be used for evil.

H: Oh, yes it can! We are not asking for God's direct intervention here; we are using a power which ALL humans have in some degree or another. If your object is 'a mountain of gold,' then this is a real thing; focus on it as central to your will (intention) and the death of some 50 or 60 million South American Indians can soon be rationalised. 'It was necessary because they stood in the way,' 'it was necessary because they were recalcitrant,' etc. All these, plus defences drawn from philosophy and theology become simple, if the focus of intention is strong enough. Plenty of people don't need objects as extravagant as 'mountains of gold' in order to kill or hurt others. The $300 in the convenience store till is enough for those desperates who focus their intention on 'my next fix.' 'My next fix' is a real object, more readily obtained than 'a mountain of gold.' It is not necessary that the object be good - only that it be real!

G: That is a chilling thought, but I guess you are right; otherwise the great atrocities of history would not have been possible; some, one or more persons, must have formed the intention, and then made it possible.

H: You are thinking again about the Holocaust. This is very fashionable, but it was not the worst atrocity in history. But enough of this, you don't have to worry about other people's intentions, only your own.

G: As you know, Henri, I often doubt my own motives.

H: It is impossible for a human being to do anything with unsullied motives; this is especially true of embodied souls. As well as what you would call the 'bodily appetites and passions' there are intellectual appetites and passions; sloughing off the body does not remove these; in fact many souls find these intensify when the body is no longer a distraction. But don't get caught up in the old problem (that is no problem) that somehow we are spirits trapped in a body.

G: But isn't that true?

H: Not really; certainly the embodied state and the disembodied are very different, but this doesn't mean a difference of superiority or inferiority. They are just different states. Some people (philosophers and theologians, mostly) who say this state is a preparation for that other state. This is not true; each state is a good-in-itself to be enjoyed and accepted joyfully; both states have their rewards and their frustrations. These frustrations and rewards arise out of ourselves, and the various influences acting on us, and how we respond. We can be sour and bitter disembodied spirits just as easily as we can be in the embodied state. One virtue you have always undervalued is the virtue of courage. I mean you have undervalued it intellectually, even though you have displayed it many times in your life; you are half-ashamed of this; you shouldn't be, think about this! I think its time we ended this session if that's O.K. with you?

G: Thanks Henri, as usual you have given me plenty of food for thought.

H: But not for worry, I hope. Relax and let go, sleep well and be kind to yourself, farewell."

September 2000.
Guillaume asked me how much cash I was taking for my eight day trip to Korea as part of a 'thank you' from the Korean Buddhist ex-veterans of Korea Association.

I told him, around $45.

He said with some consternation, "With that amount you won't get out of the country."

I replied, "It's all paid for, accommodation and meals by the Korean Buddhists. I'll be OK. In any case, that's all I have."

Unbeknowns to me, he mentioned his concerns about my finances to Henri, who organised $600 to come to him as mentioned in the prior session. He generously gave me half, $300; so I went with $345 to Korea; had a wonderful trip; spent it all.

The Korean people were overwhelming with their gratitude for those Australian soldiers who fought over there. I inquired why they were so thankful to us while they patently disliked the US military personnel stationed there. One Korean put it this way to me, "You Australians helped us then went home - the Americans stayed on."

I remembered Korea only as treeless, broken and barren country, all blacks, greys and browns from the intense and continuous bombing and shellfire. Amazingly, the Korea I saw on this occasion had been transformed into a garden, coloured in every imaginable shade of green from the crops bottoming the valleys, to the greening which rose up every slope clothing every mountain side in verdant colour.

It was a good gut feeling to see these present day luxuriant panoramas pleasantly replace my old memories of dark greys and dismal browns; all of which was a rather grim back-drop to the many homeless refugees fleeing shell-pocked cities, towns and villages.

Korea is now a successful thriving country. Too much so some might say, for on one night over there our bus often slowed down to virtually a standstill because of the amount of traffic jamming the wide highways in the heart of Seoul; and this at after midnight.

To have borne witness to all that abundant change which had taken place over two generations was simply amazing. Ah, but I digress.

Al cap des set ans vedrego le laurel

CHAPTER VI

The Fourth Dialogue.

July - September 2000.

H: "Greetings, Guillaume!

G: Hello, Henri; its unusual for you to start me off.

H: I think its time we talked about some of the virtues we discussed in earlier sessions. Do you feel up to it this morning?

G: That's great, Henri. For someone who hates philosophy and theology you certainly give them a good run.

H: I know, I know ... but your pre-occupations must take a prominent part in my discussions with you; and don't forget that I'm only interested in real things, not total abstractions like Justice; I'd rather deal with specific cases and ask questions like 'what is the fairest thing to do in this situation.'

G: I know that, Henri. I think we're getting to be more on the same wavelength as time goes by. What did you want to say about 'the virtues'?

H: I realise you are familiar with the scholastic definitions of the virtues and their breakup into natural and 'supernatural'; a lot of that derived from the Greeks, especially Plato and Socrates, as well as Aristotle, of course. But there is a list of things which Christians are regularly taught which have never been classified, even by Aquinas et al. as virtues, but which are commonly accepted as being either virtues or virtuous states by most Christian apologists.

G: I'm trying to think of an example; I guess that meekness and humility are two that come most readily to mind. In fact, casting my mind back, I do remember questioning my Novice Master about those two, as well as poverty and obedience. These were never classified as virtues by the classical writers, either pagan or Christian. Can you think of some others? The Novice Master told me they were 'functional Christian virtues.'

I was told, in the nicest possible monastic way, to take the sceptical look off my face. I had long forgotten that; but you are right, one does tend to think that meekness and so on are virtues, but when one meets a very meek person one finds them excessively irritating. In fact thinking back, of the thousands of priests, monks, bishops, etc. I can't think of too many of them who were meek or humble ... hmm!

H: I like that ... 'functional Christian virtues' indeed! Lets think of a list of these virtues or states: being meek, being humble, being poor, being exploited, being cowardly, being subservient, there are others but that will do to start with.

G: I see your point, but 'being exploited' ... is that one fair?

H: Servants, obey in all things your masters according to the flesh... Knowing that of the Lord you will receive the reward of the inheritance: for ye serve the Lord Christ. (Colossians 3.22-4). isn't that a recipe for an exploitative relationship between 'master and servant,' as the relevant legislation still describes the status of employers/employees?

'Pie in the sky' is the best bargain that employers have ever struck. In fact, a very good case could be made that Christianity has its greatest appeal to the powerless and inadequate. We should be pursuing a path which leads to your fullest empowerment, Guillaume, not one which leads to servility or submission to anyone or anything.

G: Not even to you?

H: Cheeky wretch! Particularly not to me.

G: Can't resist my little joke.

H: Go for it! As the current expression has it. I enjoy a little ribbing.

G: I suspect you would have been an irascible man, in the flesh.

H: I had more than my share of 'appetites and passions', and I'm happy to say that, on many occasions I enjoyed them to the full.

G: *Je ne regrette rein*, eh?

H: I'll forgive the flaky French and get back to the subject. It is a frequent 'Christian' attitude to say things like, 'I'd rather live in the Western Suburbs, the people are more real' - what a load of rubbish: Christians are few and far between, in the flesh, but their long-lived attitudes have infected many, many people with an underlying set of self-destructive values; just as your laws are still based on so-called Judaeo-Christian ethical systems. This is not necessarily bad, but the combination of Roman Law, Canon Law and Military Law with the Judaeo-Christian ethic has provided your country (Australia) with a mishmash of legislation where the good of individuals is subordinated to some grand idea of 'Justice.'

G: Many good ideas have come out of this system though; it could be argued that democracy had its roots in the Christian concept of the equality of persons.

H: Someone once said, 'I can't hear what you're saying because your actions are speaking too loudly.' ... or, if they didn't then they should have.

    Does the hierarchical structure of Pope/Cardinals/Archbishops/Bishops/Priests/Deacons supporting a structure of Emperor/King/Lords/Knights/Gentry/Squires/Yeomen and vassals speak as loudly to the canaille as the few quotes from the New Testament, of the type you mention? In fact, even in their essence, people are not equal; in their abilities they vary even more widely. Nature gives some men strength, others weakness of limb; some women beauty and grace, others, sadly not; some intelligence, others stupidity ... I could go on. What everyone is entitled to from others is equal respect; this is important to the giver of the respect rather than the object, however.

G: You are a tough man, Henri.

H: I've been called that before; maybe I'm too tough, but you could do with a little more expression of the fire in your belly at times.

G: Whoops!

H: I mean it; you have too high a regard for many of these Christian virtues; a sort of sneaking regard for them - at least as concepts, even though you find them repulsive in practice. I'd like to be even tougher for a while by applying what we're talking about to you; I won't do it unless you agree. Are you tough enough?

G: There's only one possible answer to that! Go ahead.

H: The reason Matheus has a female guide is that he needs a little gentling; the reason I'm here is because you need a little toughening. Until now you have kept me on abstractions (which I dislike) despite my best efforts, do you agree?

G: I know ... proceed.

H: I'll deal with a few abstractions and then get down to bedrock You won't like it! Have you ever wondered why alcohol is so attractive to you? Of course you have; and a right old farrago of nonsense you've built up to explain it: genetic inheritance; addictive properties of alcohol; need for fellowship, and so on.

The simple truth is that alcohol and Christianity are brothers under the psychological skin. By drinking, or by adopting Christian attitudes, you cannot only refuse to face problems and responsibilities, you can actually assert that the problem is no problem. It is even possible for you to see yourself as being 'good' or 'in a state of Grace' when you actually shelve or walk away from your problems.

Christians and drunks really want the fulfilment of success but are not willing to do the hard work, how easy to compliment oneself on lack of achievement by looking to the Beatitudes, or by drunken showing-off with mates (strangers are even better, you can lead them on).

In our minds and hearts we know what is wrong with ourselves and the situations around us; drinking weakens our desire and will, to do anything about these problems; Christianity has the same effect by supplying a false rationale for our inaction. Either drug will do to either excuse inaction, or to give it a suitable 'spiritual' agenda.

What would it be reasonable for a man to hope for in life?

What would it be reasonable for you to have expected from life? ... sexual fulfilment, creativity, money sufficient to give you sensible freedom of action, some position in the world, good friends and a ready acceptance of life's inevitable challenges?

Now, thankfully, you weren't drunk all the time, nor were you Christian most of the time, so some of these things came to you; but you have limited and hamstrung yourself with these two 'drugs'. This is not the path of a strong and intelligent man; nor is self-destruction with tobacco. It is no good puling and crying about your addiction; you know that you could stop smoking with an effort ... so what if the effort is great. Don't worry, you will stop: either voluntarily or involuntarily. It is impossible for you to justify this behaviour any longer.

Don't fashion a hypocritical credo for yourself which you know to be bogus. Whatever you truly want can be yours, self-mastery being principally amongst your wants, isn't this so?

G: You're really socking it to me this morning.

H: Don't shrug me off with a false jocularity. Let me give you a quote; 'A 'Christian' perspective is not limited to members of the Christian church; it is for Nietzsche, a permanent psychological possibility. We all become Christians when we profess indifference to what we secretly long for but do not have; when we blithely say that we do not need love or a position in the world, money or success, creativity or health - while the corners of our mouths twitch with bitterness; and we wage silent wars against what we have publicly renounced, firing from the parapets, sniping from the trees.'

G: As you know I had to knock off this afternoon because

I was going out with Dieter, I went over to Concord and waited for him. I gave him his birthday book *The Consolations of Philosophy*. I went to the lavatory when I returned to his office he was browsing in the book. He asked if I'd read it and I said, "No," but I had looked up the bibliography. He was much amused and, knowing of my former Christian commitment he read out to me the exact passage you quoted this morning. When I questioned him, he explained that he had looked up the references to Nietzsche (being a fellow German) and had come across this passage.

Over dinner, at the German restaurant in Balmain, I told him about my communications with you; as he has always professed to be a rationalist and a sceptic I expected him to react adversely. To my surprise he took it all in his stride.

H: We'd better stop there; I know why you are excited, but it is now after midnight so we'll call it quits until tomorrow (or today rather). Goodnight Guillaume; calm down, you can tell me all about it then. Sleep well and relax."

CHAPTER VII

The Fifth Dialogue.

July - September 2000.

G: "Hi, Henri, welcome to a continuation of our last conversation.

H: Always glad to listen to you, Guillaume; though I must confess I do most of the talking. What would you like to discuss?

G: I wanted to talk about the night out I had with Dieter.

H: I don't think we should. I know you are breathless with excitement because you have not yet learnt to accept miracles; you are on the way to expecting miracles but are hampered by the explicitness of your expectation; by all means expect miracles but do not try to pre-formulate them. You are not God; I am not God. We are less than children faced with the Divine; yet within us, there is the Divine Spark; we are not God but within us is the Immanent. So we must expect miracles but cannot, without presumption, say what miracles will or should come to us.

G: You seem very different today.

H: I'm aware of my responsibility to allow you to be yourself; so from time to time I must withdraw my didactic responses to your questions. You realise that there is no ultimate end to this process. Let me express to you why I must not constantly adumbrate and explain. In the end one explains away everything; having made nothing clear. You must experience reality; but its interpretation and absorption into your soul is your duty not mine. I know I am puzzling you, but let me say this: real meaning hovers always at the edge of consciousness. You are waiting for me to stop so you can say, 'please explain' or 'give me an example.' I won't do this, but I will give you a series of images which you can take with you to your secret room and ponder; remember that meanings are never isolated, but come in congeries and clusters:

The man is walking down into the valley; the day is hot but not stifling.

He ponders the question of meaning; what does it all mean?

There is a stone in his sandal. He bends to remove it. Why am I wearing sandals?

He pushes on, down into the shallow valley. Where am I going? What is the meaning of my presence here?

The stubble crunches beneath his feet. It must have been dry here for some time. Despite this the valley looks fertile. It is only his feet, feeling the ground beneath the sandals, which speak of dearth and drought. Why is this so?

He looks up and sees a solitary bird flying in the same direction as he is moving. The bird is black. It does not draw away from him. It does not fall behind. It beats its wings valiantly, it is a big bird, very high: There must be a strong wind at that height. Why is it flying so high and so urgently? Why is it flying alone?

A slight but pleasant breeze springs up. He comes to a quietly rilling stream. This is the spot to wash his feet. 'Hello, Dad.' A little boy of four or five stands on the other bank. 'Why do you call me Dad?'

'Because you are my father.' This is a perfectly satisfactory answer. Why does it puzzle me?

The man thinks of this while he watches a dragonfly hovering over the reeds. Its wings are transparent. Its wings shimmer, from time to time, with incandescent colours. 'Why do the dragonfly's wings shimmer so?' I don't know son.'

He dries his feet. He crosses the stream. He takes his son's hand and they walk together. 'Why are your feet dry Dad?'

'Because I dried them.'
'But then you walked across the stream.'
'So I did.' He is puzzled himself.
'Will I be able to do that when I grow up?'
'What's that son?'
'Will I be able to walk on water?'
   He does not answer. What answer can he give without raising false hopes? Did I walk on water? My feet are certainly dry.
   The child is distracted. 'Look at the bird.'
 'Where, Bill?' He has suddenly remembered his son's name.
 'Way up high, the black bird.'
 'Oh, yes I saw it earlier.'
'Dad?'
'Yes Bill.'
'Why is it flying so high?'
'1 don't know son.' They walk in silence for a time.
   The little boy looks up again. 'It's still there, Dad. Why is it flying in the same direction as we're going?'
   Having no answer the man remains silent.
'Why Dad?'
 'Why what son?' Bill explains with strained patience;
 'Why is the bird flying in the same direction as us?'
 'There is a reason, but I don't know it.'
 'Is it true what Mum says?'
 'What does Mum say?'
 'She says' you can't put an old head on young shoulders.'
 'She's right son.'
 'I'm going home now Dad.' He scampers off.
   The man trudges on. He ponders the old saying; 'you can't put an old head on young shoulders.' How does he explain to his son the turmoil of mind and body in adolescence? How does he tell him of love? Would it help if at a suitable time, he said, 'One day you'll love a girl the way you love your mother.' This would be a lie; love has different meanings depending where we are in our experience.
   He turns back to follow his son. He must explain that there are

67

things he knows which he can't explain; not because he doesn't know them but because he knows them from a depth of experience his son doesn't have. How can I tell him of the pain of betrayal? My betrayal of others? Others betrayal of me?

He comes again to the stream. The dragonflies still hover, wings shimmering. One is sitting at the tip of a reed, motionless. As he walks around it he notices that the wings change colour from red to blue to mauve. The colour of the wings depends on where he stands. Have the wings no colour, then? Has experience no meaning? Do we give the wings colour? Or is the colour dependent on where we stand?

He goes to cross the stream. He remembers his son's question about walking on water. Did I walk on water? As he puzzles over this question, trying to remember how he crossed, he realises that this is no stream but a mighty torrent. What will 1 do? Dare I try to cross this violent and turbulent water? His questions fill him with fear.'

H: Do your questions fill you with fear, Guillaume? We'll leave it there for now."

CHAPTER VIII

The Sixth Dialogue.

July - September 2000.

G: "You gave me plenty to think about the last time we spoke Henri, I begin to see the deeper truth you are trying to convey to me. Is there some particular aspect I should be focussing on?

H: No, Guillaume, but I would like you to think about the nature of what Jews and Christians describe as 'revelation.'

G: 'Revelation' in general, or as it relates to those two religions?

H: The concept in general, but with special reference to those two, because you know them so well. They, along with Mohammedanism, are archetypically 'revelation' religions. Hinduism and Buddhism are two 'revelatory' religions but in a very different sense. The 'revelations' of the Old Testament are very clear and unmistakable; unmistakable as revelations, I mean. *The Book of Genesis* starts off by telling the creation myth of the Jews; it does not tell you where this story comes from, nor who is the writer. I don't intend to do a blow-by-blow analysis of the texts under discussion but, rather, I want to make a point about revelation, including our conversations and Matheus's with his guide. As I was saying about Genesis; it doesn't take long to introduce God as a character (in fact, an active participant) in the drama of the tribal life of the Jews. Indeed, he is frequently quoted in direct quotation - as saying this and that. Later, He goes as far as to write down His own words in letters of stone, on two tablets, now unfortunately lost.

According to the scholars the first three books of the Old Testament were written by Moses. God's commands are incredibly detailed about day-to-day life for a tribe on the march through a desert. In that context they make eminently good sense: don't eat shellfish; don't eat pork or any product of the pig; don't cook meat in milk; and so on. There are over nine hundred commands about such matters in these first three books. Some are given as much weight today as in that time; many others have been allowed to slide quietly into disuse, except by the most fanatical. 'The Law' is a far more comprehensive entity than the Ten Commandments. As the books of the Old Testament proliferate, the references to direct utterances by God diminish markedly, until the last few books (as arranged by the Rabbis) where He seems to disappear altogether. The New Testament is a different stew of fish completely, and we'll discuss that later: with particular reference to that most unique of books which closes the New Testament; namely *The Book of Revelation*.

The author(s) of the Old Testament, whoever they might be, are clearly telling interesting tales, with very disparate sources. For example, in *The Book of Kings* we get the lively (and entertaining, as well as psychologically revealing) tales of Saul, then David and Saul, David and Goliath, David and Jonathan, David and Bathsheeba, etc. This is clearly not intended to be revelation; rather it is an exposition of what is seen by the writer, as a significant period in Jewish history.

They may, or may not, be 'true history' in the modern sense, but they are clearly stories from the folk history of the Jews. They are also attempts to reinterpret the history in the light of subsequent events. In other words the author is saying, 'we are such and such a people now because of the way David behaved. We owe much to him and his son Solomon, but ... the Kingdom wouldn't be divided now if everyone had acted on Jehovah's instructions; there would not be idolatry now if ...'

A lot of the books are this type of hindsight writing, and are clearly so, to any clear minded reader. The important thing about the Old Testament is that it clearly places the Jews at the centre of world history and Jehovah as an active participant in this evolving history. This is one reason that so many modern Jews find great difficulty in accepting and understanding the Holocaust; was it a punishment from Jehovah? Was it a totally random event? Does it have any meaning in the world of Israel, as it now is? The revelation histories of the Old Testament are extremely tribal and collective; even the stories of individuals, such as Judith, Abraham, Jacob, David or Solomon, are told with particular reference to the history of the people: the lessons drawn or not drawn; the warnings heeded or not heeded, etc. Interestingly, the punishments, too, are collective. Even the unfortunate aboriginal occupants of what becomes the land of Israel, are punished terribly, just for being there!

The method of worship undergoes drastic revision as the history of the Jews progresses. Poor old Cain has his burnt offering rejected, because the Lord God prefers the savour of burning meat. But later prophets are exhorting the people not to sacrifice animals, but rather to bring clean hearts, forgiveness and good intentions to their worship; though dearly, as we see in the New Testament, the practice of sacrifice continued into the Common Era. The Voice of the Lord God is not heard near so much in the New Testament. Salvation, here is an individual thing and is dependent on good behaviour, good intentions and, above all, charity, love for one another. The voice of Jehovah, when mentioned in the New Testament is heard as a 'voice from Heaven' or is an oblique (sometimes direct) quotation from the Old Testament

There is a coyness about references to the God of Israel, Yahweh (Jehovah); suddenly he is My Father or Our Father; almost as if he were a different God. And yet ... curious disparities arise.

The fig is blighted because it is not bearing fruit out of season ... is this an echo of the unreasoning anger of Yahweh? There are other inconsistent (in a character sense) incidents in the New Testament You might like, for your amusement, to catalogue them ... not a necessarily useful activity.

G: That is a pretty thorough job you've done on the Bible.

H: Not my intention, that's not at all my intention in this discussion. I am talking to you about the nature of 'Revelation'; let me deal with the most interesting of the 'revelation' books in the New Testament, namely the book that bears that name: The Book of Revelation. It is a striking contrast to the three Synoptic gospels, yet does have some stylistic echo in the Johanine gospel. It is, of course, traditionally attributed to the author of The Gospel of John. It is said to have been written in a cave on the Greek Island of Patmos; this hasn't hurt the tourist trade to Patmos one little bit! It doesn't matter though, who wrote it nor where it was written. It carries certain hallmarks which show it to be the work of a mystic undergoing an experience of the Great Mystery. Very interesting, and I will return to it, after looking at a few other 'revelation' texts.

The oldest of these is probably the *Bhagavad-Gita*. It tells a story clearly and sequentially; in the process it reveals the nature of 'God' (Krishna) and man (Arjuna and other characters). The story is simple and straightforward; it says what happened; it relates what Krishna said; it tells us how Arjuna responded. It is a 'history' in the same sense as the story of the Flight from Egypt or the tale of David and Goliath: It does not have the 'otherworldly' quality of some of the books of the Old Testament, and it is a million miles away from the mystic images of *The Book of Revelation*. But it does have the strong narrative and didactic thrust of many of the Old Testament books, and the Synoptic gospels. Why these similarities and differences?

Before the *Gita* come the *Vedic Hymns*; these are remarkably intense and poetic; they have seen much scholarship expended on them in an attempt to explain them. They are mystical, poetic and very beautiful; but they are not of the stuff to 'convert' the common man, nor to explain to him his place in the world. The first three books of the Old Testament are obviously about a society in transition; the books are a guide to the path to follow in this period of change: also what happens to backsliders! These Old Testament texts are clearly social documents, and have socially and morally didactic purposes; they also serve to give a theological explanation of the world/man/God. The *Vedic Hymns* have more in common with *The Song of Solomon*; they are passionate and filled with love, expressed in human terms, even though obscurely.

The Koran claims direct revelation from God (via an angel); once again with strong social control overtones. There is no doubt that this book inspired the great cultures of the Caliphates of Baghdad which so impressed the Crusaders with their obviously superior learning. The inspiration persisted into the Ottoman Empire but as something more ossified and sterile, eventually dying from a sort of internal suffocation.

The books of revelation persist into modern times: the Mormons with their book written on sheets of gold (sadly lost like the Jewish tablets of the law), delivered by an angel; the various more modern 'channelings' of the words of Jesus; no doubt these 'revelations' will continue as long as man is man. Perhaps I should say, as long as man undergoes mystical experience and then defines it into his current political context, in an attempt to give the Mandate of Heaven (to use the Chinese term) to his, no doubt, personally overwhelming insights.

The mystically powerful *Book of Revelation*, the *Vedic Hymns*, and the writings of many mystics are in a different category altogether from other 'revelation' literature. *The Book of Revelation* depicts a horrifying picture of Apocalypse; fire, sword, disease, disruption of the universe and eventual destruction. John (or whoever) was clearly a mystic overwhelmed by his close personal approach to the Great Mystery: some would say that he shows an evilly retributive God at work. We are too prone in the West to separate Good and Evil and, even to personify them, as I have just done with my capital letters. Our philosophers then define God as Creator, Good, Beautiful and True (all abstractions). The Theologians (sometimes the same person e.g. Aquinas) then have the problem of evil to explain; a 'Good Creator' who has created a world in which the qualities of 'evil, ugliness and lies' flourish alongside the (to us) more desirable goodness, beauty and truth: But back to the more mundane matter of our communication. You are at no risk of believing that this is anything other than a one-to-one human conversation ... correct?

G: Correct; though I was extremely startled at first and had many reservations. Now it is as if you were an aspect of myself, though psychologically very different in many ways.

H: You wrote poetry in your younger days under the influence of, or as a response to, the 'Oceanic Intuition' (as some psychologists call it), or the 'Unitive Experience' (as it is called in Mystical Theology). You know how extremely difficult it is to sculpt the huge marble block of mystical experience, into the elegant shape which, intuitively, you know it contains; you know, too, the real disappointment of the failure to convey the reality into words. People who have shared the 'God-grip of the Universe' (as you once called it) recognised what you were attempting to say; even though they dismissed your literary forays as 'tritely verbose.' All this should make it easy for you to see the varieties of source of 'revelation' texts and be able to distinguish them from our communications.

G: I get your point precisely. That is the longest burst you have ever given me, I think.

H: The point is important, Guillaume. You have enough experience and are knowledgeable enough, not to be carried away with the idea that somehow you are getting messages from

God, or some very important angel, or some such delusion. Our communication is easy and human; that is the fundamental fact. In addition, you can now understand better, what are the sources of the various 'revelation' texts with which mankind has deceived itself to the point of mass-murder.

G: The three types of text are derived, if I understand you correctly, as follows: straight-out folk histories (with or without a didactic purpose), ecstatic and inchoate responses to the Unitive Experience and, most dangerously, specific commands or directions purporting to come from God, directly and, in some cases, with incredible detail.

H: Fair enough! You are a great classifier, Guillaume. Irritating at times, but quite useful, in some circumstances. The important issue is that my words to you are for you and about you. They are not meant to be normative for all mankind; I know you don't risk making that interpretation.

G: No, I don't; but I have sometimes detected a change to the somewhat more 'mystical' mode, the more formal diction one associates with what you call 'revelation' literature.

H: Astute of you to pick that up; formal diction … I like that. Some purported 'channelings' have an embarrassing, and obviously bogus, seventeenth century speech pattern; like a cheap 'historical' movie. You have a better sense of self than most people. You surprise me. I thought most humans had a strong, too strong, sense of self. Isn't that so? Let me show you one view of mankind. It is possible to see people more as vague, flickering points of light; points of light which illuminate small stretches and threads, at intersections of a web, a network of humanity itself. Much of this web remains dark and shadowy; not necessarily untenanted but occupied by dark, unlit or dim spirits: also by the unknown dead, the spiritless dead, still there but obscure, dark and dismal. I speak of a total view unfamiliar to you. In this view we are not ourselves; we are all part of a whole which has meaning in itself, its own meaning; we, the individuals are merely points on a curve, crossroads, meeting-places; we can't exist independently because we are only signs, groupings and conjunctions.

G: I have a much more robust sense of myself than this; what you say is quite foreign to my way of thinking. It seems rather horrible, to be honest!

H: You would be surprised how many people would find my description quite applicable to themselves. The herd instinct is not only present in grazing animals but in many, many people; a highly visible threat is ignored because of that feeling 'there's safety in numbers.' After all, only one or two of the outside animals are caught and eaten. The parallel is not exact, I speak only metaphorically, but numerous folk ignore their spirit, their mind and feel that the body is them. Few accept the concept of the spirit (or soul) in charge of the mind and the mind in control of the body: we must accept that the body is an innocent being, controlled by the mind and spirit. This raises the question, why do we punish our innocent bodies? We punish it with ascetic practices for 'spiritual' reasons, we punish it by neglect, we punish it for ego gratification; in fact, mankind has found numerous reasons and ways to punish the innocent body and an even larger number of ways to blame it for evil.

G: That's very true, Henri.

H: I mention it because it is an important motif in your life; at one time *fortissimo*, but now, much more a *diminuendo*.

G: Is that really so?

H: What short memories we humans have: penances, false (but punishment - invoking) confessions, austerities, monastic restraint, marriage ... need I go on?

G: Why did you include 'marriage' in the list?

H: Because I wanted to discuss it with you - but only if you agree.

G: O.K. I'm game.

H: Your view of your marriage with Elizabeth is a distorted one and you need, I suggest, to examine it more closely. If you agree, then it is up to you to do this but I am going to give some direct, objective facts about events and your reactions. Still so game?

On second thoughts I think I'd rather leave it for the time being. I think I'm worried by the 'demons' that I'd have to face."

Wednesday, 13th September 2000.
I had coffee with Guillaume. He said that he was again communicating with Henri who wasn't pleased with the energy he gave to the Korean Veteran's Association.

I agreed.

Guillaume told me I had a mention during the last session. Henri told him to tell me that after my next birthday on 1 November 2000, the disruptive influence of the recalcitrant 7 in my date of birth would cease; all those difficulties which have plagued me up to this time throughout my life, including my chronic lack of money, would cease.

I must say that my life did change dramatically. During my entire life I had never won a raffle or lottery apart from once winning a set of golf clubs; unfortunately, I didn't play golf. Since that birthday in November of 2000, it seemed I was winning something most every week.

I moved into a new apartment surrounded by trees; consequently, I was awoken with bird song every morning; yet still living close by the city. I went from being a dancer, to a dance teacher, with attractive female students lining up to be taught. Life had indeed dramatically changed for the better. The many failures of the past had become merely memories for memoirs.

CHAPTER IX

The Seventh Dialogue.

Friday, 6 June 2003.

H: "You should know something about 'money in abundance' now.

G: I do thank you.

H: Its not a question of thanks. It is about perception.

G: I know, you have made the point that my idea of abundance is correct viz. that abundance is a relative term.

H: Yes and no. Let me ask you a few questions, O.K.?

G: Go ahead.

H: What was your feeling about the $3,600 when you collected it? Think carefully.

G: As I had only $45 in my pocket and $430 in the bank, delighted! I was delighted.

H: Did it seem like abundance?

G: Yes, it did.

H: At what point did it seem like abundance? When the meter ticked over? When the girl wrote the ticket? Or when you collected the cash?

G: I am sure that it was when I was putting it in my wallet alongside the $35 there. I remember that I was thinking that now I could leave the $430 untouched in my bank account and when the next pay went in I would be over the $1,000 mark in my current account. I was planning to put $200 or $300 back into my 'special' account of the $1,000 I had taken out in Perth.

H: When you won the $360 did that seem like 'abundance.'

G: To be honest I was stunned. It didn't scent real until I collected the $1,000 cash: That really seemed like 'abundance.'

H: When I invited you return to the roulette wheel on Tuesday after our big win why did you resist me?

G: I suppose that I was treating you as if you were a friend I had been doing this with and you just wanted to go on for fun I guess.

H: Be a little more open with me. You pretended that you were resisting an inner compulsion to gamble, didn't you?

G: Well I have known people who have gone on to disaster after a big win on the horses. They suddenly get a keen interest where there was little before. My friend Tony is an example. It wasn't financial disaster but psychological that he suffered.

H: We'll return to that at some time. You were surprised when I suggested that you put $5 in the machine?

G: Yes I was. I thought, what's the point?

H: Do you see the point now?

G: I'm not sure that I do really. I guess you were making the point that you could do it again.

H: Did you? Tell me what you were really thinking.

G: Frankly I thought you were showing off, in a sort of a way.

H: Were you surprised when the number 17 came up as I had suggested?

G: I was very startled. But it seemed pointless, in a way. Like piling Pellion on Ossa. It seemed pointless.

H: Tell me 'frankly' in what way pointless?

G: You could have instructed me to put $50 or $100 on. Then the win would have been $1800 or $3600.

H: Did the $180 seem like abundance when you had collected it?

G: Not like abundance, more like icing on the cake. When I opened my wallet it was filled with money already.

H: If you had won this money on Monday afternoon would

it have seemed like abundance to you at that point?

G: Yes, I think it would.

H: I leave you to think about that. Let's return to your idea about disaster resulting from abundance.

G: That's not what I said.

H: No, but that's implicit in what you did say. This brings me to the next point - respect for money. What do you think of that idea?

G: Money is a two-edged sword. It makes people arrogant. It leads to disaster because of drink (e.g. B.U. perhaps) or because of gambling or women (e.g. Ray) or the lust for power (the Toad).There is no end to the damage that could do. I know it can be used for good, but it is more often used wrongly. I think I respect money properly.

H: I think you have shared some of your fears and reservations about money. I'd like to discuss some of these points with you.

G: Go ahead.

H: You say money is a two edged-sword. Isn't that true of everything?

G: I think everything is putting it too strongly. There are many wonderful things like a mother's love what are not two-edged; the love of humanity, too; the compassion for others; the beauty of the Universe; the majesty and goodness of God. I could go on.

H: Yes you could go on. In fact you carefully guarded your tongue and your thoughts as we communicated. You thought of a list of good things which you rapidly discarded; water, electricity, fire, and sunshine, amongst others. But you saw straightaway that these 'good things' had the two-edged quality you give to money almost exclusively. You thought 'drowning,' you thought 'electrocution,' you thought 'burns,' you thought 'skin cancer' and discarded them to make a debating point. You are a formidable protagonist, my friend Guillaume, but we know one another too well by now for these games. Admit that you put money (or at least 'abundance of money') into a special category of things to be careful about.

G: You could be right.

H: I don't want you to just say 'you're right' without understanding all the implications of your thinking. This is one of the serious roadblocks I spoke to you about on several occasions. Do you mind if I ask a few more questions?

G: O.K.

H: I don't want you to be sullen or resistant to the ideas we will expose together. Please comprehend that I am devoted to your good. But when I said 'everything is a two-edged sword'

I meant everything I do not exclude myself from this. Respect is the great defence we have against this double quality in everything. Do you agree?

G: I'm not sure yet. Ask your questions. I'm sorry, I'm doing my best not to be devious with you.

H: Do you remember what you did after you went for your Doppler test yesterday?

G: I went for the test at 8.30 a.m. and it was finished at 10.00 a.m. Then I paid a couple of bills at the Post Office and I went to the club for lunch.

H: What were you thinking?

G: I thought I'd check the machine I'd won on so I'd understand better how it had paid so much money in one spin.

H: What else were you thinking?

G: I wondered whether you would suggest that I play again.

H: When I didn't respond what were you feeling?

G: I was wondering whether I could be so fortunate again.

H: You avoided the word 'lucky.' But you didn't play it; you walked away when the lady asked if you were playing.

G: Yes I was tempted to play it again. It would have been nice to win again, but I did realise eventually that my wins of Monday and Tuesday were not a question of 'luck.'

H: Why did you wait for me to speak? Why didn't you ask me if you should play again?

G: I thought I was being greedy. It didn't feel right to ask you when I had no immediate need.

H: You must reread this with Matheus later. There are some very revealing comments in what you've said here. You need to share these thoughts so as to come to grips with this fear you have of money. Fear and a deadly attraction, are not unknown as a combination. I would like to see them replaced by a sensible respect for money. Your are not alone in thinking this way; there are subtle and important differences between you and our friend Matheus, but you do share some very serious roadblocks. It is not my job to help him, but perhaps these discussions will do just that.

G: I'm happy to do that.

H: I'd like to return to some of the things you feel are not two-edged. You mentioned a mother's love. Is that never two-edged, seldom or often two-edged?

G: I get your point. Mother's love can be destructive.

H: I would like you to think about that very deeply before our next conversation; also think about the fact that you didn't mention a father's love. Think about those things please. The love of humanity, you mentioned that too. Do you remember our talk about abstractions?

G: I get the point. To save you the trouble I'll admit that there again I've given abstractions qualities they can't possess.

H: Do you even admit that about 'the goodness and majesty of God?'

G: I'm not sure now. I can't see where that could be a two-edged sword.

H: 'The majesty and goodness of God' is an unfortunate theological construct which can mean nothing to you because you actually know nothing about God. Isn't that right?

G: I see that. These habits of mind are difficult to overcome.

H: Don't despair. This conversation is well worthwhile.

G: I can't help feeling that there is some subtle point that is just beyond my grasp.

H: There is a point. It's not a point I'm trying to make but rather, one you must make for yourself

G: I'm sorry, I don't think I'm being deliberately obtuse, I'm just not quite getting it.

H: You've heard the philosophical discussions about perception, especially the one about a percipient who mistakes a piece of rope for a snake?

G: Yes, that's a hoary standby. Some of the most boring rubbish is talked about this change of perception. It comes into the same category as the standard examples like the vase or two heads depending on whether one focuses on the fore- or background.

H: Exactly. But returning to the snake/rope example. When the percipient sees that the snake really is a piece of rope, that doesn't mean that now there is a snake that has slipped away and is lurking dangerously about the place.

G: Of course not.

H: Don't be annoyed at the simplicity of my argument. The point is - there isn't a snake, there never was a snake.

G: That's definitely true.

H: You are trying not to be annoyed with me. Why do you think you are feeling annoyed or insulted on precisely this little detail?

G: Are you trying to say that there is 'abundance' but I'm not perceiving it?

H: Yes, but that's only partly it. I'm trying to get you to change your perception, not just recognise that you have a misperception.

G: Please explain that a bit.

H: Well, I'll propose the hypothetical case of a very nervous girl who sees the rope, thinks it's a snake and screams hysterically. Her father comes along, 'See Sue, it's not a snake, it's a rope.' She now perceives that it is a rope, but the fear and hysteria were real and when she goes to bed she has a nightmare about snakes. In time these events fade from her memory but it is possible that a residual fear of ropes lingers.

G: So what you are saying is that I have a fear or hatred of money?

H: I'm sorry to say that is not the breakthrough moment. Do you think you value money too much or too little?

G: Too much, I suppose.

H: I'm going to ask you to do something that may annoy you, but please do it. Take a break and calculate how much you spend a fortnight on cigarettes. I'd like you to do an honest and accurate calculation.

G: I've done the calculation. At the best price in Bankstown I spend $249.20 a fortnight.

H: And you don't always get the best price so quite possibly you spend $255 or $260 a fortnight?

G: Yes, I think you're right.

H: Do you remember that the Dept. of Veteran's Affairs wrote to you to get you to fill in a 'Lifestyle Questionnaire'?

G: Yes

H: The suggestion in the letter was they were considering increasing your pension from 100% to 150%. How much roughly would this have given you as an increase per fortnight?

G: About $125 a fortnight. I know what you are going to ask - yes, I was excited at the prospect.

H: You said that you thought you valued money too much: Think about whether that's true, in the meantime I'll ask you about an incident that occurred in Chapel Street in Melbourne about six months after your mother came over. Do you remember the incident, please spell it out for me so we can discuss it.

G: You are referring to the man I gave money to?

H: Yes, I would like the details so we can discuss them for your benefit and for discussion with Matheus perhaps, if that's what you choose to do.

G: I was staying with my nephew John and his wife J. We were driving around. I had an appointment to meet a few people in a restaurant in Chapel Street. We drove in from Eltham and their eldest son came with us. We were in the St Kilda area and Jr. (the son) wanted fish and chips so I bought some for the three of them. We went down near a pier and they sat in the van eating. Sorry about this detail but it has a bearing on what I subsequently did.

H: This is good, go on.

G: John got out of the car - probably to ditch the scraps. Jr. and I were alone in the van. I asked Jr. what he wanted to do when he grew up. A stupid question that all uncles (or granduncles for that matter) seem obliged to ask 15 year olds. He was sitting in the back and he replied 'Nothing, I don't want to do anything when I grow up.' He was so vehement I was shocked, 'But you can't do nothing. How will you live?' He said; 'I don't care. I'd be quite happy to be in a cell in South Melbourne lockup, naked, just so long as people left me alone.' I took the hint and shut up. John drove me to the restaurant. Jr. and I said nothing with mixed emotions, but mainly with an awful fear for young Jr.

H: I'd like to come back to that at another time. I'd like you to recall what your emotions were and the series of events leading up to giving the money away.

G: I had been a bit embarrassed in the fish and chip shop because I'd had to give them a $100 bill, but they had been able to change it without fuss. I had the change in my trouser pocket - probably about $70. 1 was standing there looking in the fashionable shop windows thinking about Jr. and I said a prayer for him. Then the thought came to me that as an act of penance for him I'd give away this money to the first person who asked me for money. Then I thought, 'that's not very likely, not in this affluent place. Chapel St. is a very upmarket district.'

H: What else were you thinking?

G: Not much, I don't think, it all happened so quickly.

H: You were also thinking about your nephew Jr but we'll return to that in another context, but please go on.

G: Only a few minutes after I'd had the thought, a quite well dressed man approached. You must know the street was very crowded as it always is on Saturday nights there. This man had a truly desperate look in his eye. He started off by saying, 'I have never done this before, but I'm in desperate need and I need help.' I said to him, 'I've been expecting you. There is no need to explain. Here, take this.' He was very surprised to have all that money shoved into his hand. 'Thank you.'

G: 'Don't thank me just say a prayer for Jr.' Just then my friends showed up and the man went away.

H: You've thought about this often haven't you?

G: Very often.

H: Would I be right in saying that it puzzled you a great deal?

G: A very great deal. Of course I thought about the man quite a lot, speculating on what his problem was...

H: Let's stop there for a moment. You never let him explain his problem, did you?

G: No, but it was obvious to me that he was about to ask for money.

H: Maybe he wanted you to tell him the way to the next street?

G: Please Henri, don't joke.

H: I'm not joking! Perhaps he wanted advice as to the nearest counselling service for suicide. Perhaps he wanted to know where he could buy a knife at that time of night because he wanted to stab his unfaithful wife? There is an endless list of possibilities of what he might have been about to say, but you cut him off.

G: That's true.

H: And now when you think about the incident, these and similar speculations enter your mind?

G: Yes.

H: Now, a very important question. Did you act out of compassion for the man?

G: I suppose l did.

H: Now, Guillaume, consider this: you had decided to give this money to the first person that asked you. A man emerged from the crowd and began to ask you for something which, you assumed, was money. So you gave him the sum you had predetermined to give away. That is a fair summary, isn't it?

G: Yes, it is. But I'm fairly sure that he was going to ask me for money, I gave it to him to save him further embarrassment.

H: But you gave it out of compassion for Jr. didn't you? You had determined on this course of action in response to Jr's extraordinary statement, hadn't you?

G: That is exactly it. I felt that it would help Jr. somehow.

H: Now I know you well enough to know that this series of questions will aggravate you, but I intend to ask them anyway. You said you decided to do this as an act of penance for Jr. What 'sin' had Jr. committed?

G: None really, but it was a sort of denial of life.

H: Did you think this act would somehow 'placate the Furies'?

G: That is very insulting. I'm not a Greek, frightened to name spiritual entities.

H: Did you think you were placating 'God'?

G: Probably.

H: Did you think 'God will strike him down for saying that?'

G: O.K., O.K. I wasn't thinking very clearly.

H: You are getting very tired and we have opened up some serious areas for discussion. I hope you will transcribe your scribble so that you and Matheus can discuss this together, if that's what you wish. I'm sure you realise that this is best kept between the two of you. The insights that will surely come should not be diluted by the inane, yet powerful, input of other people's scorn. If you discuss this with others they will only cement you back into positions that are comfortable and familiar to you.

In a very important way this is a solitary struggle, you struggling with your roadblocks, Matheus with his. Discussion between the two of you may be helpful to both of you; but in the end you each struggle alone, because your problems are similar but subtly different.

I would love to see money pour into your lives, but it will never come in 'true abundance' while the barriers are up against money.

G: I don't really know what to do. I've got some inklings of what you are trying to uncover in me but I don't know what I can., in a practical sense, do about it.

H: I'm going to make a suggestion which, after your conversation with Matheus, you may decide to adopt. Is that O.K?

G: Yes, of course. Anything practical will be a relief. This has been a very gruelling exchange for me.

H: I think the better word might be 'painful.' I'm not sorry about that. Surgeons don't cry while they are cutting out a diseased appendix. It would be best if you wrote these words down more slowly so you get them right. They are not some magic formula but the ideas expressed should be clear and unambiguous.

G: I'm ready.

H: You know that I've never suggested any type of prayer to you, I'm not going to do so now. What I am going to do is give you a set of words to repeat to yourself. .... I emphasis that these words are addressed to yourself.

Please underline that last sentence. They are not addressed to me, or 'God' or some unknown 'life force.' They are addressed to you and may help in keeping your mind focussed on the subject of money so that you will come to understand the roadblocks that have been erected in you, by others and your interpretation of your life experiences in the light of what you have been taught. I hope this is clear to you.

G: I think so. You are going to give me a set of words to say. This is not a prayer. It is not addressed to you, or God, but only to myself.

H: Exactly!

G: How often should I say these words?

H: As often or as seldom as you wish: This is entirely up to you. Without becoming obsessive about it, I think you might say them as often as the thought occurs to you, not just when you are in need. If you do it when you are in need, and only then, you are indicating to yourself that this is a prayer. You should not be asking for something, but acknowledging a reality.

G: I've got all that. Ready when you are.

H: This is the form of words:

'Money in abundance is now coming to me in a perfect way and I treat money seriously and with respect, accepting what it can and can't do'.

G: Is there anything else?

H: I know how tired you are but let me make these last points. Most people treat most important things 'seriously and with respect' because they have not been given a distorted view early in their lives. For instance, most people treat water seriously, they know that they can drown, but they have no fear of this with a glass of water.

Have you ever wondered why a game of poker played with matches is 'less fun' than when played for money? Is the game 'fun' or is it the possible win or loss that is 'fun'? Does money have some mystical value for you? Does money say something about the people that have it? These and other questions may occupy your mind? Enough for now. Try repeating this form of words after you have had your yarn with Matheus."

CHAPTER X

A letter from Guillaume.

Saturday, 7 June 2003.

Dear Matheus,

Hello young dancer! This letter is to welcome you to your new home, to tell you a little of my trip to WA and to give you the precise details of what happened last Sunday, Monday and Tuesday.

Welcome to your new home; I hope that you will be very, very happy in this place. When you think about it, isn't it surprising how it worked. If you had a reasonable neighbour in your first placement you would still be there: cramped-up and limited. As it was, the very thing that made your life unpleasant for a year or so was the very circumstance that justified your upgrade to a unit you would probably never have achieved, in any case welcome. I hope to see the place when you have properly settled in.

I've told you a good deal about my trip to WA, what I would like to tell you about here is the adjustment I quickly made to living at Falcon with Bill. He could not be faulted as a host. He wouldn't let me do anything he made my coffee, he washed and ironed my clothes, in short he was like a kindly mother. Being an ungrateful bastard I sought ways to avoid this for a time each day. I found that Falcon Bay Beach lay about half a kilometer to the East over a couple of hills, and The Estuary lay about a kilometer to the West. So every day (or almost every day) I took a book for a walk, sometimes to The Estuary and more often to the beach, for two or three hours of solitude. The beach was very beautiful, with the added amenities of a coffee shop, lovely lawns and shelters adjacent to the sand and a viewing point on the southern end of the beach on a small promontory. From this vantage point I could see for many kilometers - a further beach down South and a good sweep of coast to the North

On some days I had earnest conversations with Henri. Much of these were just about me and would bore you, but one thing he did say to me was that 'money in abundance' would be coming, that there were no external roadblocks to this, only my own thinking. Of course I later began to think and analyse these words. I'm sorry, Matheus, but that is the way I've been trained (conditioned?) to think. Now on to the events of last Sunday, Monday and Tuesday.

Last Sunday, 2 June.
I was thinking about Henri's promise that there would be 'money in abundance.' I began to discuss this with myself. A million dollars would not be 'abundance' to Kerry Packer and a billion dollars would hardly be 'abundance' to Bill Gates.

On the other hand 100 dollars would be abundance to a poor fellow living in a cardboard box. As I was indulging in these cogitations about the relativity of such qualitative words as 'abundance' Henri joined in pointing out that, "My ability to know about money was much cramped by my contempt for it."

Much of that discussion I will tell you about later. And so to bed on Sunday night.

Monday - 31 June.
I had to go to Bankstown and by 2.00 p.m. I had not had lunch so I popped into the bistro for something to eat, which I had in my favourite corner of the plastic rain-forest. I began pondering the previous night's ruminations but Henri did not join in. When I left I was walking out when a new digitised roulette

wheel caught my eye. Henri suddenly joined me and said, "Put ten dollars in."

I reluctantly did this as I had only 45 dollars on me. Henri said, 'We'll have a little bet, just wait.'

So I stood there for a while watching how it worked. Each player has a console to himself. This console displays, inter alia, the time left before the wheel spins again. With twenty-seconds to go Henri said, "Put the ten dollars on number 26."

After a few seconds confusion I did this. The ball spun and twenty-six came up. The 'credit meter' suddenly counted up to $360.00. 'Call the attendant.' So I did and after 5 minutes wait a girl came along and wrote me a ticket, which I then took to the Cashier. All this ticket-writing etc took about five or six minutes. I collected the money and went home. When I got home I had $395 in my wallet. To say I was stunned would be an understatement. Indeed I even suggested to Henri that I return and repeat the performance. Henri was dead-set against this. We had a lengthy discussion about respect for money. And so to bed on Monday night.

The next day I had to meet you at 11am. and take some dry-cleaning to the shop. I arrived at about 10.20 am. at the club. I was sitting in the lounge near the door when Henri said, "Let's go for a walk!"

He led me up and down the rows of machines and suddenly said, "Stop here, put ten dollars in this machine." There was confusion about this, but someone pointed out that a ten-dollar bill was acceptable to the machine. I put the ten dollars in, pressed the buttons suggested by Henri. I was horrified when, after the first spin, I realised I was spending $2.50 per spin. I knew it was stupid, but I pressed on, fully expecting to lose the ten dollars. On the third spin I won something. It was 15 free spins. During these free spins money accumulated in the credit meter. By the 13th spin $75 had accumulated.

I was delighted. On the fourteenth spin the machine began to go berserk. While the machine played music I worked out that we had won 20,000 credits ($200). But the credit meter continued to roll on and I realised that two substitute symbols were on display. One of these said x3 and the other said x5. This meant, I worked out, that the payout then in progress was going to be $3000!!! Despite my doubts this proved to be correct. When the free spins were over I had won $3079.50. More correctly, I had won $3069 - taking into account my initial outlay of $10. I pressed the button for the attendant and got my ticket for $3079.50.

I returned to the lounge to wait for you. It was still only 10.45 am. Henri said suddenly, "Let's look at the roulette again."

I was in some doubt whether it was Henri and not some gambling lust that had overtaken me. Henri left me in no doubt. To cut a long story short, I returned to the roulette wheel. Put in $5 and waited. On instruction I put the $5 on number 17, which duly came up. I collected the $180. I asked the Cashier about my ticket for $3079.50 and she said, 'I'll have to call the Manager for that.'

I said I would come back later - I was anxious not to miss you. I had only been in the foyer a few minutes when you came.

Interestingly where I had $45 in my wallet on Monday afternoon, by the time I met you I had about $580 plus a ticket for $3079. It was interesting, too that the Cashier paid out my $1000 in 10 x $50 dollar bills and 5 x $100 dollar bills. This clear division of the thousand dollars was of obvious significance to me (Guillaume was instructed by Henri to give me $1,000). The rest you know. I am still getting over the experience and have some conversations to report to you when we meet next. I think I am understanding the nature of 'abundance' and also something about 'true respect' for money. I don't know if I can see you in the coming week. I have appointments on Tuesday, possibly on Wednesday and/or Thursday so Friday 13th June seems the earliest. We'll be in touch during the week anyway.

Your somewhat shell-shocked mate

Jim (Guillaume).

I, Matheus, after arriving at the club and enjoying coffee with Guillaume, he surprisingly handed me $500 saying, "I was told to give you that by Henri!"

After lunch, when Guillaume went to the cashier's counter to collect his winnings, he was advised that he could only take $1,000 in cash, the balance would be paid by cheque. Henri again suggested to Guillaume that he give me another $500. So I walked away from the Club with $1.000 which allowed me to register my vehicle.

CHAPTER XI

The Eighth Dialogue.

Friday, 20 June 2003.

(Additions downloaded from Guillaume's computer files which are an incomplete Dialogue).

H: "I'm sorry about the negative thoughts that seemed to be the essence of our last conversation.

G: No worries. I have really derived a lot of benefit by opening these old wounds. I've always realised that my feelings for Elizabeth were very complex and contained the key to my understanding of, and my relations with women. I'm very grateful for the insights I got from our conversation. I hope that today we can discuss the form of words you gave me previously to share with Matheus.

H: I thought you might like to get down to some practical discussion. You are talking about money, am I right?

G: Yes, its been a fortnight since we had the long discussion about money and the spectacular demonstration you gave. I'd like to understand better what it all means.

H: You are finding this conversation very awkward aren't you?

G: Yes, I feel that way because I don't want to seem too eager about money I guess.

H: I'm going to disappoint you for a while. I will discuss the question of money but I'm going to do something first which I have always steered you away from.

G: O.K. You have me intrigued. To put it bluntly, what the heck are you talking about?

H: Well, I always tried to steer you away from your propensity to bog down in philosophical argumentation; but I'm going to indulge myself in a bit of that now before we get down to what you think are more practical matters.

G: I know that money is a mundane thing, but that's what I thought you were going to talk about.

H: Yes, but first of all I want you to understand something of the nature of phenomena. None of these ideas are new to you, I'm going to present four ideas for you to examine the ensuing conversation by. The first thought is 'almost all phenomena you, Guillaume, experience, are impermanent, subject to constant change.'

G: I don't know why you qualify that idea with the word 'almost.' Surely all phenomena are subject to change?

H: Not quite all. The nature of the phenomena you perceive is constant change. You even look at yourself and say 'I have changed.' All your observations are correct, except the last one:

The 'essential you' does not and cannot change.

The essential you is overlaid by the various 'I's' that we have discussed before.

G: You are losing me somewhat.

H: All the phenomena you observe are really composite (made up of various parts or elements) things; they are not reality. This applies even to the 'I' that you perceive and call yourself. All composite things are contingent and therefore impermanent – subject to change. One time you say to yourself 'I am angry'; another you say 'I am happy'; another time again you say 'I am sad.' This is the 'I' you identify with at any one time. But this is not the 'essential self' that is the real you.

G: You are saying that I am really a group of different 'I's'?

H: Not at all. You do what everyone does, to a greater or lesser extent. You respond to external factors by saying 'I am angry' or 'I am sad' or 'I am happy.' You can't be simultaneously angry, happy and sad, can you?

G: That's true. I suppose when I say those things I'm really identifying myself with a passing emotion or state of mind.

H: Worse than that, you feel that this is permanent. For instance, when you were so desperate and unhappy about Elizabeth you were immersed in this role for four or five years. You've seen others in this 'immersed' condition, Jr. for example.

G: You seem to be suggesting that I act out a 'role' merely playing at being whatever I am at that time."

The remainder of this session missing.

CHAPTER XII

The Ninth Dialogue.

15th July 2003.

H: "This is a true history of the universe and man's place in it. This will only be a partial truth, not merely because you would not understand but because I don't understand everything myself. As I've constantly told you, I'm only human and also because I am still partly contaminated by matter.

Let me start by saying that everything comes from The Source. I don't want to enter into theological discussion, but some references must be made that will seem theological. I would prefer that you accept them as simple statements of fact, rather than starting points for endless dissections for hidden meanings.

Who or what is The Source? That is a natural question for you to ask. The answer is I don't know. My teachers have used different names for The Source… The Ungrounded… The Essence… That Which Is… The Light … and many more. Many great religious teachers in the flesh have given names to The Source, and I must digress here to explain something very fundamental. How does Truth become contaminated?

The Contamination of Truth.
The worlds of matter and the spirit are inconceivably different from one another. Man is a combination of both; at his core he is a Spark of The Source: this is man's essence. But man is not only

a spirit, he is a spirit immersed in matter and the movements of his mind, which are fleshly, are often confused with the still 'voice' of the Spark.

Many mystics, poets, philosophers and artists have perceived or experienced something of this 'voice.' They then try to convey it to others in practical terms and confusion arises. The simplest example I can give you is the well-known story from the Jewish Bible of Moses' dialogue with The Source. Moses asks for the name of this voice that speaks to him and the voice responds by saying, 'I AM.'

Moses was a political and tribal leader and he uses this astounding revelation to impose hundreds and hundreds of rules and regulations on his tribe in the name of 'I AM.' The revelation becomes enmeshed in his mental activities and he proceeds to give out what he considers good advice in the name of the Great 'I AM.' This becomes The Law.

'I AM' is as good a definition of The Source as it is possible to give in human terms. Consider the implications of the Ultimate Godhead saying, 'my essence is that I exist.' In a very real sense The Source exists uniquely.

Moses' difficulty is firstly understanding this himself and, secondly conveying it in a meaningful way to his tribe. Man's first response to knowledge of the Spiritual World is to turn this knowledge into laws for others. I am talking to you in the almost forlorn hope that this will not happen in this case.

I know that you have no political aspirations, no desire for control of others and no wish for spiritual domination. So the worship that ensues is not worship of The Source (which, in any case, is not required) but worship of something else which we will come to later."

The remainder of this session missing.

CHAPTER XIII

The Tenth Dialogue.

7th August 2003.

H: "Dear Guillaume,
How sweet is the communication of souls, but how difficult it is to describe the indescribable. I am a spirit not in the flesh:

You are a spirit embedded in the flesh and find it difficult to understand except in the prison of matter. You must not take anything I say as a condemnation nor as an exaltation of you or anyone or anything.

The most important thing we might learn together and go on learning together is this:

Things just are. As they are.

So I embark on this endeavour to explain some of your deepest questions. How is it possible? I can only speak of the high and deep things of the spirit by metaphor and analogy, by similitude and resemblance. An example of what I am saying is the difficulty we have in describing taste. What does an eel taste like? We say like a chicken with a fishy overtone .., or whatever fanciful simile we can conjure up, but the only way we can know a taste is by experiencing it.

The first question I must address is the origin of all things. As I tell you the truth in metaphor you will form mental images drawn from your previous experiences and thoughts. All of

100

these will be wrong. I would like my words to come to you in the deepest recesses of your soul and resonate there in some approximation of REALITY.

The Source of all things is The Source. The Source is also called the Light, the Ungrounded, and a myriad of other names. I do not use the word God to you because you could not help but impose on this word a host of images. I want your concept of The Source to be untainted by previous theological ideas. Even words like 'the Light' conjure up images of the sun or candles, and so on.

If I call The Source 'Light' then I must tell you at the same time that it is a light of the most unspeakable darkness.

If I call The Source 'Darkness' then I must say in the same moment that it shines with the most refulgent and resplendent light.

It is, in fact, impertinent to speak of The Source as-it-is-in-Itself. Only The Source knows Itself. Viewed by us, whether in the flesh or in the spirit we can only look at the completely unknowable within any meaningful sense of the words. All I can say of The Source is that it Is. It is being-itself.

A light separated itself from The Source, at this moment time, space and matter came into 'existence.' We form no judgement of this. We cannot say 'this is good.' Nor can we say 'this is bad.' We cannot say 'this was willed by The Source' nor can we truthfully say the opposite. This separate being we call the Artificer, because the Artificer is the creator of all things that are not The Source. The Separation is the origin of man's struggle. The reason for this is clear. Despite the separation of the Artificer from The Source yet the Artificer remains of The Source, and everything created is, in its deepest self also from The Source. Embedded in man is something of The Source - a Spark from The Source.

The Artificer, by nature and origin, cannot help but convey a Spark of The Source into everything created; when I say everything I mean the Universe, the stars, the planets, everything both animate and inanimate. The Spark, so deeply and invisibly embedded in all things, yearns for reunion with The Source. It is the deepest yearning of each Spark to return to The Source.

Baldly stated, I have told you everything and nothing. I have also told you nothing new. Many ancient traditions have knowledge of these facts. Where we have gone so sadly astray is in ascribing a human 'morality' to them. Do not think that I am saying that morality has no meaning; on the contrary it is absolutely essential that man develop moral codes. I will return to this later.

What we have spoken of to this point concerns things utterly beyond human concepts such as 'good and evil' or 'right and wrong.' It has nothing to do with reason or logic or science. It has only to do with ... what is! But mankind is tempted to judge all things from its own perspective. Think for a moment how limited that perspective is and how individual too. The farmer yearns for rain, the city dweller hopes for fine days. The child wants it to be next week when its birthday is due, the lover wishes it were yesterday so that words spoken might be unsaid.

As well might we judge by the perspective of other creatures. What of the perspectives of the lion and the gazelle? The oak and the woodworm? The bacterium and penicillin? We could go on. The Divine, the Uncreated are beyond all our judgements. But with some inkling of the knowledge mankind have labelled The Other as God or Devil or Angel or Demon.

Others, more philosophically inclined have given names of commendation or condemnation to certain aspects such as 'active' or 'passive' or 'malignant' or 'benevolent' - a vast host of judgmental terms. Unfortunately I must use the language available to us and use some of these terms from time to time, but I do so out of necessity and without praise or blame.

I have expressed myself as simply as possible and have attempted not to give grounds for some doctrinal system; the world has had enough of doctrine, enough of arguing about things that are only dimly apprehended. Rather, having given a concept of the central fact of the Separation I would urge you to consider this:

> *The role of every Spark from The Source*
> *is to return to The Source.*

This may sound like a complete discarding or overcoming of the Self. This is true, but only in the sense that what we look on as our 'selves' is not really our individuality. Humans are multi-layered in their being; both in their conscious self and in the spiritual layers. At our inmost core is the Spark from The Source: the light within. Then there is the layer which comes from the Artificer; this too is from The Source but, because the Artificer has, by will, created matter and immersed the entirety of Its being in matter, this layer (so often called the soul) is attached to matter. It is at this level that I communicate with you. This soul is what we mistake for ourselves.

Our true individuality lies within the Spark from The Source. When we finally reach and are reunited with The Source we become more ourselves, I will say more of this later. For now I will tell you something of the Cathars in answer to your questions.

Since first the Spark entered mankind it has been discerned by each individual that internal conflict exists. This conflict is between what is called the Soul and the Divine Spark; mankind finds it easiest to escape temporarily from this internal conflict by externalising it. The greatest conflict has been with matter: the capture of food, the killing of enemies, dominance over other members of the tribe: failing this, finding a place in the communal pecking order.

It is at this point that the concept of morality enters. Transgressing the standards of the society is now taboo – 'sin.' In the order of matter it is not possible to reconcile every need. One has more than another and the transgression of theft occurs.

One lusts after an unwilling female and the transgression of rape ensues, and so on. For social reasons and for the rationale of power, more and more possible crimes are added; as a consequence more and more penalties are piled up. Death for not knocking the forehead three times on the floor in the presence of the king, for example. True crime is the invasion of another's rights. Because the Spark exists in every human, then every human knows when real error has come into his/her life. The more deeply immersed in matter the soul is then the easier it is to defy the Spark, or even ignore it.

Within matter everything is contingent. If I stub my toe on a rock then the toe is hurt. If you own that thing then I can't own it. Being material means to be contingent at every moment and in every material situation. From mankind's first beginnings the struggle has been with contingency. We have discussed this so often, but let me now give you this simile:

Mankind is immersed in contingency as a fish is immersed in water; it is so all pervading, so much the medium of our human life that we are only dimly aware of the generality of contingency.

We take for granted this condition, which actually is merely a condition of matter. Now my soul is not enmeshed with a body you might think that I am freed of contingency; not so, because contingency will only fade away as the illusion it is when my Spark merges again with The Source. The Cathars understood this and considered all theological 'knowledge' and doctrine to be without any meaning. They perceived this and understood that at the level of the soul these and other concepts such as morality, reason, and human love had some validity. They wished for and struggled to achieve reunion of the Spark with The Source. This made it easy for them to acquiesce in any theological proposition put to them by their Inquisitors. So many things are true of the soul and have no relevance to the Divine Spark. The real positions of the Perfecti were profoundly threatening of both Church and State, and were seen as such by both the Cathars and the authorities to be so. These doctrines were about reunion of the Spark; they were not about salvation of the soul.

Please understand that these insights were not peculiar to the Cathars. Many great mystics from many different traditions had intuitively understood this knowledge. The teaching of the Perfecti were not well comprehended by the majority of the Cathars; but the people did know that the Perfecti were different from the many clerics who tried to govern their lives. Some of these clerics were important nobles who had enriched themselves with the benefices of the Church; the majority were ignorant and their Latin as barbarous and confused as their 'teaching.' So what was the pure teaching of the Perfecti?

Dion, the greatest yet most obscure of the Cathar mystics taught that humanity was made of matter; the nature of matter is that it has components, or parts, unlike spirits which are unitary and indivisible. The components of man are the sensible and visible body, the sensible but invisible mind, and the sensible soul, which directs and informs the mind and body. These components are all products of the Artificer. But there is something else which is the essential man and cannot be considered as a part because it is the Divine Spark; the true reality 'individuality,' if you like, of man is within this Spark.

 In order to free (rather I should say 'realise') the Spark; in order to reach 'Perfection' - you see how difficult it is to say the unsayable? In order to reach Perfection, the soul must be deeply engaged with the work. The soul, which is the most spiritual part of man, must pass through darkness that Dion calls the 'night of the soul.' Dion points out that the soul has two aspects: a sensual and a spiritual aspect. Both must be purified by a process, which might be described as a voyage.

The first part of the voyage is the purging of the sensual soul;

the second stage of the voyage involves the purification of the spiritual soul. The soul cannot embark on this journey unless the Spark within draws it. It cannot, of itself, even discern that there is a path ahead.

The first step is detachment, or withdrawal. This has been much misunderstood.

It is wrong to say that detachment consists in the abandonment of all material things; material things are not, of themselves, attachments.

Attachment lies in desire. You may possess all material things and be detached. You may possess very little of material things and yet be attached strongly by desire.

It is not material things which keep the soul occupied and injured by things of this universe, but rather the desire of, and attachment to them. Not all desires are equally harmful to the path:

Not all desires confuse the soul in the same degree. There are natural desires - that is, natural in the flesh - which do not, of themselves, harm the voyage of the soul.

The natural movement of the soul towards these physical desires need never be a bar to the reunion. The annoyance and distraction they cause may remain entirely in the physical realm while the spiritual soul desires only reunion.

Nevertheless the sensual soul must be corrected by compassion. Compassion has been much misunderstood. Compassion is the yearning arising in the spiritual soul for the Spark within; the Spark not only within oneself but also within all mankind. True compassion lies in this yearning. Things done for other bearers of the Spark can express this compassion. If done with the sensual aspect of the soul then they are seldom true compassion, but self-aggrandisment.

The ultimate state of Union lies in this; the total obliteration of what we perceive as our will as well as immersion within the deep darkness of the Light of The Source.

The first step of the journey is into the night of darkness by the sensual soul. This is a night of the senses.

Meditations and other spiritual means may be used to begin the process of purification. If prayer is used then it should be directed to The Source. Simple aspirations of a few words or wordless sighing of the sensual soul are sufficient.

When embarked on this course the first steps are the movements of the bodily senses.

It may be that the soul and body experience a certain sweetness and delight.

The sensual soul delights in all forms of music, art, laughter and happiness. There are many consolations and much happiness available to the sensual soul. These are not to be despised, but to be enjoyed and passed over.

All souls who experience these joys of the senses in the first steps of the spirit are drawn by The Source. Sadly, many stop at this point of the journey. It is as if a man who had lived all his life in a desert, knowing only the joy of an occasional oasis, heard of a great sea so huge that it was beyond his wildest imagination, who sets out to reach this ocean. On the way he comes on a large pond. He delights in it and disports himself. Time passes and the water becomes muddier and less pleasant; his delighted joy begins to fade. At last he wearies of this pond and returns home. He sadly tells his friends that there is no great ocean. He is the man who having tasted the spiritual delights of the sensual soul returns home and says, 'There is no Source.'

The soul has this sensual aspect in which the delights of the spirit may in a small part be found. These delights should be treated like a fruit plucked on the path; enjoy them as you walk but do not believe that they are the end or purpose of the journey. While purifying the sensual soul by means that come to you, turn the will at all times to The Source.

It is in action of the will that the sensual soul is cleansed for the journey into the spiritual soul.

It is during this time that the sensual soul should be turned by the will towards the darkness (or light, if you will) of faith:

This faith should lie first in the guidance given, or if not given, then expected and eagerly anticipated

Secondly this faith should be in The Source and in the dark path that leads to reunion.

Faith should see reunion as the goal, never daunted by the apparent impossibility of the task. Faith is the spur and goal that should force the soul forward.

In this night of the sensual soul some light still lingers. Reason and thinking remain and these are not blind. It is at this point that the journey into the spiritual aspect of the soul truly begins.

This second part of the journey requires abandonment of the reasoning faculty. The soul should begin to walk as a blind man, by faith.

The soul now experiences utter darkness (or blinding light if you will). It must abandon not only those things associated with the sensual soul but also those things which it now begins to experience of the spiritual soul.

The soul now begins, if truly drawn by The Source and its own desires, to experience spiritual powers of seductive attraction.

At this point of the journey much caution must be exercised.

The detachment from spiritual things is most difficult for some and impossible for many.

This is the stage of the passage where very many stop. Who has not been seduced by the powers now revealed

Attributing these directly to The Source is wrong. They are only powers that arise from the spiritual soul; they come ultimately from The Source but are the proximate work of the Artificer.

Every human has these spiritual powers. Many creatures have spiritual powers derived from the spiritual souls appropriate to their species.

In most humans they are submerged and neglected. These faculties can be developed and enhanced but should never be considered as the aim of the voyage. They are as incidental to the journey as the delights of the sensual soul of which I spoke earlier.

It must not be thought that these faculties of man are in any way strange or peculiar.

As I said before they are a function of the spiritual aspect of the soul. They derive their power from their proximity to the Spark.

Here I will digress and discuss these powers as you asked me to do. Mankind has a certain faculty or capability which it has submerged in the ever more complex world of matter. Primitive man, still close to his origin in the Artificer had this capability. Let us merely call this Capability S (for submerged). One of the signs of this Capability is the ability to heal by touch or thought.

Capability S becomes apparent in some that have entered upon the path to their spiritual souls. This Capability can be developed and exercised.

Serious exercise of Capability S should be prepared for each day. Firstly there should be a short period of meditation to engage the sensual aspect of the soul with compassion; the Capability should be exercised with the greatest humility and never for material desires

This does not mean the grateful recipients of the healing should be denied the expression of gratitude by material things. Material reward should not be the desire or purpose of the healer. It may result incidentally.

So the daily preparation for the healer should begin with a short meditation on compassion; the compassion is for all that are separated from The Source.

Experienced healers should then abandon meditation and enter into the darkness (light) of the spiritual soul. At this point a quiet simplicity should enter the awareness.

There should be no seeking after signs or wonders - but they will come.

The capability you are willing to express this day is yours planted in your spiritual soul by the Artificer, but ultimately from The Source.

Without words or images and in deep quiet and silence of the spirit blindly look upon the brilliance of the darkness of The Source.

Without words or images and in deep quiet and silence of the spirit listen for the silent music of The Source.

Without words or images and in deep quiet and silence of the spirit listen for the musical silence of The Source.

It often happens that some physical reaction occurs at this point; this is caused by a movement of the spiritual soul which impinges on the sensual soul and hence the body.

The most frequent reaction is a sense of heat in the healer's abdomen; but many other physical reactions may occur.

When the healer approaches the one to be healed he should make a short withdrawal of the mind from everything but compassion; compassion for the fellow-sufferer of the Separation.

Sometimes the healer places hands on the sufferer; any movements should be unpremeditated and spontaneous, under the influence of the spiritual soul.

The healer almost always feels something goes out from him to the sufferer; the healer feels a temporary lessening of himself.

This is purely a reaction of the senses.

The more the healer perceives himself as a bridge between The Source and the sufferer the more effective he will become. This is sufficient for now on the subject of healing.

When I digressed, I was speaking of the point where the seeker enters into the work of the spiritual soul.

The sensual soul having ignored the sweetness and delight offered by the sensual aspect of the soul must now learn to ignore all the things pertaining to the 'spiritual life' and even all thoughts and images of The Source.

The soul must at this point become detached not only from the material attachments I spoke of earlier but now must detach itself from what it considers the holiest and most high things.

It is at this point that the mysterious workings of The Source will take place if it is to take place at all.

Whatever material gifts it has, the soul has become detached from already.

Now it must detach itself from the spiritual gifts that have developed within the spiritual aspect of the soul. Now it must detach itself from all images and ideas about The Source and all other things.

The soul must now be blind and without guidance from this point. The soul must lean only on the staff of faith: Faith that The Source exists and is drawing it forward.

If the soul relies on any knowledge, insights or feelings of itself, then it has not embarked on this step of the journey.

All of these things are completely unlike The Source.

All these things, though spiritual, are as much illusion as are all the works of the Artificer, beautiful as they may be.

Your senses, both physical and spiritual, are made by The Artificer for the enjoyment of matter, the great illusion.

The Spark within you is being led to its origin - The Source.

Even when the soul passes from the body into the paradise made by the Artificer, still it should press on.

The Spark that would attain reunion must not rely on any appearance, physical or spiritual, any imagination or any of the senses but must bear constantly in the interior darkness, by faith, an acceptance of the Perfection of the essence of The Source - which it cannot ever know until reunion takes place.

At this point on the path the soul must completely and utterly abandon its own way; it must enter onto the way to The Source. Strictly speaking this is a way that the soul cannot possibly know. It must blindly stagger forward in faith.

If the soul feels it knows this path, then it is not on the way. Intense activity, in the most passive mode, is the function of the soul at this juncture.

There is little more I can say of Dion's teaching at this stage, except to restate some of the things he has said, but in a slightly different way."

CHAPTER XIV

The Eleventh Dialogue.

An explanation of Dion's teachings.

H: "This is an attempt to explain the inexplicable.

To start with we must understand that Dion, when talking of the 'soul,' is describing the most spiritual part of man made by the Artificer.

The body has senses with which it experiences the world of matter. The soul is directly connected with the body and mind through an aspect of the soul which Dion calls the 'sensual soul' but also within man is a Spark from The Source.

This Spark is direct from The Source and is not made by the Artificer. It is the 'spiritual soul' which is closest to the Spark within. But it is not right to have mental images of the Spark being within man; words fail when addressing anything to do with The Source:

Where a spiritual soul is, there also is a Spark.

With every soul, even that of one we label 'vile' or' evil,' a Spark exists. This union with a soul may be said to be 'real' because it is the Spark, which animates and preserves in being the body, mind and soul of a man.

The union or reunion that Dion speaks of is not this presence but the union of the spiritual aspect of the soul with the Spark and hence The Source. This reunion is embarked on by compassion and desire for The Source. There is a very real sense in which one could say that the union of the soul (sensual and spiritual) with the body and mind is natural i.e. a union in the material order.

The reunion of the Spark 'within' with The Source is completely of the Divine order of being, of which we can know nothing until reunion. To make this clearer one may say that all animals and living things have a soul which has a sensual aspect. It is this that sustains the life within the body and mind. In man the soul has another aspect which is the spiritual aspect. It is the spiritual soul, being closest in nature to the Spark (though vastly separate) that develops yearnings for it knows not what; but basically it yearns for its existence to be non-contingent, which can occur only in The Source.

Let me say here that the delights of the material world are immense, they seduce and lead on most souls and keep them entrapped in the endless round of existence. This is the way things are. This is not a crusade for multitudes but for individual beings.

The Cathars were not trying to overthrow the Church, nor establish a rival Church; Catharism predates the Protestant Reformation by some centuries. The aims of the two movements were as different as could be. The Cathars sought to inwardly ignore the Church completely and concentrate on the Divine Spark within. The Perfecti knew that this was a hard way and only for a few at any one time. Outwardly they adhered to the practices of the Church while believing something different. The great body of Cathars knew some of these beliefs, but mainly were impressed by the incredible compassion and healing powers of the Perfecti. Even the most ignorant peasant could see the difference between them and the priests and monks of the Church:

I wish I could convey to you the complete indifference of the

Cathars to doctrine. To them the Reformation seems ludicrous. Suppose that a hypnotist induces a subject to see a white cat; this we know is an illusion, if the hypnotist now convinces the subject that the cat is black, is this any more or less an illusion than the first one? Of course both are illusions. To fuss over doctrines, or historical facts and fictions, is to be bothered by and enmeshed in illusion. What the Artificer has created is in the ultimate sense an illusion. The nearest he has come to creating something real is the spiritual aspect of man's soul. This is the tool which man can use, if called, to participate in reunion.

When man's body dies then the sensual side of the soul dies too. The 'individuality' that man has experienced while alive, in a large measure vanishes. But there is a resonance between the sensual and spiritual soul and some memories of the lived life echo in this soul. The soul enters into a form of existence prepared for it by the Artificer; this is experienced by the spiritual as more blissful than it's material existence. But it is still an illusion.

Souls which had strong material ties experience discontent and some yearning for a return to matter; hence the endless round of reincarnation. The steps proposed by Dion are the only way we know to step off the treadmill. Of course many do not desire to do this because the path to The Source seems to be an illusion. So strong can be the hold of matter.

Many spiritual writers talk of the Will of God. They are truly speaking of the will of the Artificer. Rituals, doctrines and many material trappings are the hallmarks of the Will of the Artificer. Man finds them delightful and interesting. These become so easily the signs of power - a material good most attractive to man. It seems to man that increased power reduces his condition of contingency. This is the deepest of all illusions.

The Emperor, King or Pope on his throne has an existence which is as contingent as the poorest peasant humbled before him. The frustrations of the most powerful are the bitterest of all experiences. This is not to say 'this is the fault of the Artificer.' No - it is impossible to create a material universe that is non-contingent!

The spiritual soul by resigning itself to the Divine Source, surrendering to the Divine Light, may become reunited with The Source. By this Dion means that the soul must remove from itself every trace of attachment to material things. 'Material things' include all attachments, even things of the spirit, such as powers, insights, illuminations and gifts. Religion is an illusion, as are science, human love, spiritual delights, philosophical or theological images of God; even these writings are in the realm of illusion. The works they may prompt within the spiritual soul of the reader are not illusions.

I will speak now of what I do not know but was taught by Dion. Dion is beyond my ken now for he has passed into The Source. When he was well advanced on the path, he said, that when the spiritual soul is detached from all material and 'spiritual' things and waits in silent faith in The Source, then The Source communicates its own being to the soul.

This communication is of such kind that the soul seems to become one with The Source. It seems to the soul that it has become one with The Source, but not yet. The soul now begins to feel that it is itself The Source. Indeed it begins to enter into the life of The Source and yet retains its individuality; it becomes more and more in The Source and yet becomes more and more itself.

I know that you have many questions, Guillaume, but I would like you to ponder what I have said before we enter into that. A few remaining things I must answer before I leave you for a little while. You asked why The Source did not intervene to protect the Cathars from extinction. The truth is that The Source never intervenes in the illusions of the Artificer. Because the Artificer has made universes of matter, he has created enormous numbers of contingent beings, some inanimate and some animate.

They are all illusions when viewed from the standpoint of The Source. There is a deep mystery attached to the relationship between The Source and the Artificer. It is easy to label The Source as Good and the Artificer as Evil.

I would urge you not to do this. Man is not capable of judging this subject. Remember what was said of perspective. Remember too what was said that the Cathars did not seek to found a religion. They sought to teach the truth of the total sea of illusion in which man is immersed, and the means to ignore and eventually escape this illusion back to The Source. This knowledge is very ancient, more ancient than Hinduism, Buddhism or Christianity. Yet every one of these traditions has produced many mystics and 'saints,' 'gurus' and teachers who knew and dispersed this knowledge. In particular the Jews knew of this knowledge which they brought out of Egypt and Babylon. Scholars have labelled all such knowledge as 'Gnosticism' - sometimes incorrectly.

The interesting thing about true Gnosticism is that it is incapable of being made into a religion. Because the teaching is so high and remote from everyday 'reality' it appeals only to certain advanced souls. It frequently happens that such men attract many others to whom they try to convey this teaching. For the thousands who start on this path of self-abandonment there are only tens who continue on it to the end.

I am sorry if I have made it sound as if the Way were all struggle and pain. Of course life is to some extent struggle and pain because of the contingency I spoke of. But how delightful the life of the senses can be: dancing in the sun, laughing in the haystacks, delights in feats of valour and strength: The list is endless.

The way through the sensual soul has even greater wonders and joys. The bliss and sweetness that may be experienced here are even more seductive than the pleasures of the bodily senses.

At this stage too, it may be the soul begins to apprehend the signs that non-contingency is possible. How sweet that is to man – power. The major motive of science is power; power over the intransigent 'realities' of nature, etc.

Nothing I have said should be taken as suggesting that any activity of man is an evil or 'bad' thing. It is right and fitting that man should participate fully in the life in which he is immersed; but if The Source should attract, which it mysteriously does, then this is the way in which to respond – as best I can tell you.

The only fear you may have will be that a person reading it will consider that it is madness and delusion, or perhaps 'religious mania.' Things would have been worse, were much worse, for you in centuries gone past. Some governments may see this as subversive; totalitarian states are well aware of the dangers to their regimes. This is why such ideas were suppressed with the most vicious rigour by Jewish, Christian and Islamic communities over the centuries.

We must stop here for now. Ponder what we have written. There is much more I have to tell you. I know that what I have said may seem cold and daunting to anyone hearing or reading it. This is not the truth.

I have said to you in another context that you are not, nor are you intended to be a spiritual warrior. This is not meant to be derogatory. The balanced and dispassionate side of your soul makes it a perfect means of communication between us.

As it is I have had to constantly struggle with you to accept this communication. When we embark on the next phase of these writings (very soon) I will be giving you some teachings on the best modes of meditation and practical activity. The aim is not to revive Catharism as such but to revive the ancient truths that inspired it. What arises will be a Catharism for a different age.

You may seek definitions of many things I have said. Think about it and discuss it with Matheus. If I can I will answer your questions. I have as far as possible avoided theological and philosophical terms. I have used the word 'contingent' consistently throughout in the strict philosophical sense.

Dry as my exposition may have been, I know that you have responded with an interior acceptance; perhaps I should say; 'a bewildered and questioning acceptance.' Good, I want you to examine everything with the scepticism, which is your natural bent.

I have not wasted my efforts on you: No more questions at this stage. Until another time...."

CHAPTER XV

The Twelfth Dialogue.

Thursday, 21st August 2003.

H: "Dear Guillaume,
It is with much joy that I begin this communication to you. The fact that you have an open and sceptical mind is a great aid to me. It is most important that you consider everything I say with this spirit of enquiry.

What I am imparting to you is not some Holy Writ or new revelation. Much of the information I have given you must resonate with you to have any meaning at all, even though it also raises many questions.

Before answering these questions I will proceed a little more on the way I have embarked. Let us leave to one side the problem of self, the problem of 'what or who am I,' and consider each person as he/she experiences life.

It is apparent that every human being seeks happiness and desires to avoid pain and suffering. The experience of suffering may be in the body. In this we are little different from other species.

An animal may be well fed and all its needs met, and then it is content and relaxes. Humans understand and share this experience. But humans have much more potent mental experiences that can completely overshadow and destroy or enhance physical well-being. Animals may share some aspects of these mental experiences but it is reasonable to say that mankind's capacity for mental turmoil and anxiety, even when there is no physical cause, is much greater and even of a completely different order. Conversely it is true that mankind's capacity for joy is much greater than for any other animal species.

These two broad categories of human experience, which every human shares from time to time, lead to two broad categories of suffering - physical and mental.

The role of the mind in suffering is very important. We might say that the animal suffers physical pain in this moment, whereas humans may feel that this suffering will endure forever. This intensifies human suffering to a very great degree.

It may even mean that man's suffering is not only greater in degree but also different in kind to that of an animal. However this may be, we know that a tranquil and calm state of the mind can override various degrees of physical pain in humans. In some cases even extreme pain.

Conversely we know from observation or personal experience that a human can be physically well, and still suffer tremendous mental anguish and anxiety.

Interestingly, it is notable that some of the cleverest humans, or those with the finest sensibilities, suffer from severe mental anguish and pain.

You are asking yourself why I have expanded on these simple facts that are well known to you. The reason is that I want to start on the practicalities spoken of in my first communication. I am referring to the practicalities of meditation and the spiritual path: From what has been said so far it should be obvious that the first step for an individual should be the attainment of some degree of mental comfort and ease.

Many, many people do not attain even this elementary level of mental ease or calm, except by either harmful or at least trivial ways. The harmful ways are well known and are exploited ruthlessly by the unethical or uncompassionate. These harmful ways include gambling, alcohol-obsession, drug-obsession and sex-obsession.

The trivial means are by self-annihilation in intensive sporting or physical activity, in pointless hobbies and so on - there are many trivial ways but they fit into these broad categories. The destructive means contribute nothing to peace of mind or spiritual development. In fact they destroy it further. The trivial means contribute to peace of mind but very little to spiritual development. They are not necessarily to be discarded on this basis.

There is another method that attracts what I might call 'natural man' and that is 'the way of herding.' It is natural for mankind to have a communitarian or herding instinct, Homo sapiens is a very gregarious creature. This herding can be very destructive to the individual and a source of suffering for others outside the herd. This is a natural and proper instinct in humanity. But it can be very destructive.

Examples of this abound in history, I will mention only a few; mass political parties even in relatively fair societies, but especially in totalitarian states; mass religious movements, especially where accompanied by group displays of enthusiasm and theatrical fervour.

All destructive paths should be abandoned and one of the best ways to do this is by meditation. The first step for these beginners is meditation designed merely for the calming of the mind.

I know that you and Matheus are familiar with many of these exercises so I will not delay things by involved descriptions. I will merely say that they may include physical movements and exercises designed for this purpose (e.g. Yoga, some forms of dancing and some music, especially bells, gongs and horns, stringed instruments and so on) and also by simple meditations and affirmations. These should be designed with the express purpose of bringing to the new practitioner some of the joys of the human mind.

The next stage should be the exercise of meditations to enhance the power of the mind and bring the practitioner into an acknowledged relationship with her/his sensual soul - simply 'the soul-as-perceived.' When proper connections are made between the mind/body and the sensual aspect of the soul, the practitioner may often experience exhibitions of the capacity I previously called Capability S. It is at this point that true guidance should be given to avoid the pitfalls of this stage.

From here on the practitioner will be drawn to the spiritual side of the soul. When the path into the spiritual soul is well advanced then guidance will be offered to begin the process of apprehending, or at least acknowledging the possibility of, the existence of The Source and of a Spark of that Source being in every human. At this point no guidance is possible; the soul will be drawn into a comprehension of The Source, or it will not.

The deep contradictions (as they appear to be) of the nature of The Source will be matched more and more by the emptying of the spiritual soul of all former ideas of Self. This is a summary of the spiritual path for which I will now attempt to give some guidance that may be useful, especially for Matheus in his work for others. Your way, I think, may be somewhat different.

Let me begin at the second stage of meditation, where the practitioner begins to make conscious effort to make connections between the mind/body complex and the sensual aspect of the soul. The first steps that I have passed over will have concentrated only on the Self. This second stage on which I am beginning practical instruction is the point at which the practitioner begins, for the first time, to go somewhat beyond Self.

The purpose here is to begin changing the perspective of the mind. It should begin with a practice of oneness with all mankind. It should also begin to bring to mind the difference between the practice of introspective meditation and active meditation. By this I mean that the transformation of the mind should now be expected by the practitioner to lead to transformation of action. These meditations of the second stage should bring into the mind thoughts of the emptiness of material things combined with a deepening sense of altruism. By 'altruism' I mean a sense of concern and some degree of oneness with all mankind without consideration of self.

A useful meditation is for the practitioner, having calmed his/her mind with one of the previous meditations (which I mentioned as being well known to Matheus), should be led into a meditation where a greater use of the imagination is made. Imagination is a vital power of the sensual aspect of the soul. The practitioner should be directed, for instance, to imagine a playground full of children aged about five or six. These children are of all races and sexes.

The imagination of this should be led so that the person practicing this meditation experiences pleasure in this imagined scene. If the practitioner cannot enjoy this spectacle then he/she should not be pushed any further. A normal mature adult of some experience of life should be able to derive some pleasure from a well-constructed scene.

The meditation should proceed to a conscious perception that, apart from accidental differences, such as race and sex, all these children are the same. They are, in a very real sense, one. The oneness idea should be developed in later meditations. Later meditations should expand this idea by the introduction of less beautiful or pleasant children: e.g. some leprous, some with deformity. The sense of altruism should be enhanced as these later meditations are experienced. Further meditations should lead the imagination to adult humans, again with all the differences of race, sex, health, physical beauty, etc. All this work, because it has been done with the sensual imagination, should begin to produce in the practitioner a sense of the need to be active in philanthrophy, not necessarily by giving money or things, but more importantly, by giving time and energy to the needs of others.

I must digress here and urge that you, Guillaume should encourage Matheus to draw up a list of meditations based on these principles and outlines, and to develop them for future use, where required.

Altruism is the first step on the path of compassion. I do not use the word 'love' because it has many connotations that fall outside of compassion. By compassion I mean that the spiritual soul should begin to feel for all humanity, without exceptions. Some points of exclusion are: lack of physical beauty, gender, 'bad' behaviour, etc. The practitioner should not exclude anyone. I mentioned active meditation earlier in contrast to a merely contemplative form of meditation. Contemplative meditation is most important but not at this stage.

I will explain pure contemplative meditation later, but for now I will define what I mean by 'active meditation.' Consider a person successful in any activity: warrior, dancer, businessman, doctor, artist, etc. If they are very serious about their work they, quite rightly, spend some considerable time studying and thinking of this work. This is a diluted form of contemplative meditation. To be successful they must also practice their skill or art. The mind is fully engaged in the activity. This simultaneous combination of mind and body is active meditation. Many people practice it without understanding that this is what they are doing. This can be very satisfying to many souls and they seek no more. At least in this life.

Altruism should be sought at this stage. It is purely a human activity. It needs no help from any divine source. It does need guidance from a living expert. Guidance may also come from a spiritual guide. Affirmations may be useful at this point. Some very ancient examples follow:

'It is my intention never to be a hindrance to any living being; rather I will be an object of joy to others and assistance on their spiritual path.'

'It is my intention to bear fruit from any 'evil' done to me and that any 'virtue' I may have will bear fruit for others.'

'It is my intention to always help to dispel the misery of the universe.'

'I have compassion for all souls, and for all living beings.'

So what is the difference between 'altruism' and 'compassion'? Altruism is the desire to attain spiritual development for oneself combined with the desire to do good for all souls that come my way. Compassion consists in the gradual abandonment of self for the spiritual good of others. Compassion is a deep appreciation of the inherent sorrow of existence in separation from The Source. This should not be confused with any concept of 'salvation' for oneself. Rather it is a deep desire that all may return to The Source. Some Cathar *Perfecti* used the following affirmation:

'For all the time that matter may endure, for as long as human souls are immersed in matter separated from The Source, until then may I remain to assist others to The Source.'

When once you realise the immense courage needed to make this decision you will understand what compassion is. Such a wish may commit the soul to countless returns to the flesh over vast aeons of time and much suffering. Not all consider such sacrifice to be necessary."

CHAPTER XVI

The Thirteenth Dialogue.

September 2003

H: "I know that you experienced some turmoil after the writing of this information. Let me explain this to you. I'm sure that you have some insight into this already, but I will labour a few points. By your meditations and efforts over the years you have achieved somewhat of that which is called 'annihilation of the memory.'

Annihilation does not mean erasure of memory but a recollection of events drained of their emotional content. I intend to help you by refreshing for you some of these memories. I would not put you through this painful experience except that, by so doing, I will be able to enlighten you on several points. You said to Matheus this morning that you felt as if a pall were hanging over you. I will explain this, too.

But first I will clarify a few points, which I think were obscure to you. As I said at the beginning I can only speak of these things by analogy, metaphor and simile, because we are speaking of two different realms, the material and the spiritual.

Consider first the mind/body complex. The connection between the two has led science on a difficult dance. We know that the mind controls the body. In fact it controls the entire body. There are two types of control which the mind exerts; firstly there is the autonomic control and secondly there is the conscious control. The mind, in a normal body cannot control the reflexes, the heartbeat (except in some narrow range), the secretions of the liver and kidneys, and so on. The mind can and does consciously control the minutest movements of the limbs. But the mind is not the body. If we cut off a leg the mind is in no way diminished. In fact the mind may still sense the presence of the leg when it is no longer there.

From the standpoint from which I speak we can say that when the mind experiences the twitching of a nonexistent leg it is experiencing the residual 'pollution' of matter. When I say 'pollution' beware of thinking that I am saying something pejorative. From another standpoint we might say that the mind 'pollutes' the body, that man would be happier without the mind that distinguishes him from the animals.

Returning to my theme; the mind is so in contact with the body that it is, to a degree, always conscious of, and polluted by, the body. I used as synonyms the words 'sensual soul', 'sensual aspect of the soul' and sometimes just 'soul'. Man has only one soul; the mind is polluted by the body and the sensual aspect of the soul is inevitably polluted by the mind. When I speak of 'aspects' of the soul I might say analogous things of the mind; I might say 'the autonomic aspect of the mind' to indicate all those functions of the body which the mind unconsciously controls.

On the other hand I might talk of the 'cognitive aspect of the mind' to indicate all those functions of the mind which are used to think, reason, create debate, meditate and so on. But man has only one mind. So it is with the soul. There is an aspect of the soul that, through the mind, acts on the sense data of the mind to draw 'spiritual' or non-cognitive conclusions.

When the body dies the soul leaves the body. At that moment the body/mind complex ceases to function. Yet, just as with the missing leg, the sensual aspect of the soul may still mis-perceive the presence of the body. But the soul is a continuum, just as the mind/body is a continuum. When I speak of the sensual aspect of the soul I do not mean it is less spiritual than the rest of the soul. I am merely speaking of the connecting point between the higher 'faculties' of the mind and the 'lower faculties' of the soul.

It is important to note that, so far as we know there is no connection between the soul and the Spark. The Artificer makes the mind, the body and the soul. Some say that he cannot help but transmit the Spark at the moment of birth: I believe that the Spark is in no sense 'within'. This is a deep matter beyond my knowledge.

With these explanations (do not regard them as 'definitions' in any dictionary sense of the word) out of the way, I will trigger some of these memories by a few words and then we can consider them. You need not write anything of the conversation we have just had. Let me end by saying this:

The soul is furthest on the way when it least thinks so, sometimes it even thinks that it has gone backwards.

The soul is making the greatest advances when it is moving in the darkness and doesn't know the road, nor even see the path: Remember when the soul is traveling in this darkness and obscurity it is suffering. This suffering is preferable to rejoicing and action. It is in this suffering that The Source gives strength, whereas in activity and joy the soul exposes its own inadequacy and weakness.

In fact the closer the soul comes to The Source (or the Spark within) the darker it becomes, for the soul experiences its own frailty and inadequacy more fully. The 'eyes' of the soul are darkened by the great brightness of The Source. This light is so immense, so far beyond all comprehension, that when we are drawn towards it we are plunged into blackness. To be sure you are travelling in the right direction you must close your eyes and advance boldly in obscurity.

All comparisons with others are pointless. All consideration of others in relationship with you should be cleansed; there should be no spirit of competition. Enough for now. The pall has lifted. Next time we will discuss the details you have raised about paradise, striving after death and so on.

Farewell for now and blessings.

Henri de Nebours.

Al cap des set ans vedrego le laurel

Postscript

Monday, 8 January 2007.
Though he had been unwell for some time, Guillaume died quite unexpectedly on the 7 January 2007. He just had a new book shelf installed which allowed him to get lots of books off the floor.

After his funeral, I was to pick up his computer, however, a friend of his, Dieter, wanted to give it to a patient who had language difficulties.

He rightly thought using the computer would improve her language skills. I said I didn't mind, all I needed were the files Guillaume was working on, as he hadn't given me a hard copy because there was a problem with printing out hard copies.

Some months later, when the I received the computer, I found only a few partial files remaining on the hard disc amongst his other mainly work-a-day material as they had been written over.

Some relevant entries from my journal regarding events after Guillaume's death.

Thursday, 6 March 2008.
Quite excited at the prospect of seeing the medium Suzy again after so many years. Some months ago, a good friend Myra rang me to inform me she had accidently found out where Suzy lived. My appointment was for 2.30 p.m. I was there for two hours, an hour more than the allotted session.

My mother and father were present, as they are at every session. I taped this session and all the others as it's impossible to remember all that transpires. On this day however, I needed specific information as to whether the files were still embedded in the hard-drive. Guillaume said they were, also that I should retrieve them and get on with the book. He will help me when he gets out of the Hall of Healing, as Suzy describes his present spirit location in the world of spirit.

My Mum said I need to get my neck attended to otherwise it will cause trouble later. Suzy suggested a Cranial Spinal Adjustment which fixed her own neck problem.

On the tape, Guillaume explained to Suzy how he died. He said that on the evening of his death that he had a spitting headache. He went to lay down; not to sleep but because of the pain in his head.

He lay there for awhile when suddenly, he exited through the top of his head with a 'whoosh!' Next thing, there he was floating around near the ceiling while looking down at a body, which he said was in a kneeling position. He was somewhat confused for about fifteen minutes when he realised that the body next to the bed was his and that he was in actual fact, dead. I was told that when he was found by his brother, he was in a semi-kneeling position beside his bed.

He said the experience wasn't painful; quite the opposite, in fact it was euphoric. He gladly would have done it again as it was such a great experience; no pain whatsoever. What really surprised him was that he was looking down at his own body for quite a while not realising what had actually occurred.

Guillaume said it took some time for him to realise that he was actually dead. He then went on to say that he was met by his Guide, Henri. Not only that, but he was conversing with Henri in Occitan. He said, "I had no idea I could speak Occitan," which was the language spoken 700 years ago in Languedoc by the Cathars.

Friday, 30 May 2008.

Dieter arrived with the computer. He said he felt somewhat responsible for the files that were missing as he had reformatted the disc, thus making it harder to retrieve any residual information. I replied that Henri said, "We need to accept that 'things are just as they are'. However, easier said than done.

So the missing files are either buried somewhere on the hard drive or they're not; or they can be recovered, or they can't.

Wednesday, 11 June 2008.

I had come to an arrangement by the Data Recovery experts that if the files could be retrieved, my cost would be $1,200, but as, if they couldn't be located, the company representative said there would be no cost to me. That was the deal.

Although I had cheaper quotes from other firms, I believed that these people would do their best to locate the files rather than lose such a large amount of money; especially, after having spent some time trying to locate them.

Unfortunately, a few days later Michael from Forensic rang to say, "Sorry, but we can't retrieve any files as it is such a small hard-drive. As well, all the disc space has been overwritten which made our task even more difficult."

This was a real emotional kick in the guts for me. Nonetheless on the same day, I emailed Dieter with the sad news. I told him not to take it to heart, for whatever reason.

Thursday, 12 June 2008.

When I went to pick up the computer from Forensic, Michael said, "The hard drive has such a very small capacity consequently there wasn't much space remaining where residual pockets of information could be stashed away." True, the hard drive was only 2.8 GB capacity. By this time I was already coming to accept that the files weren't likely to be recovered.

Thursday, 19 June 2008.

A clever I.T. friend of a friend Luke, now has the hard drive to have a crack at recovery. I e-mailed Dieter to let him know what was happening. I do hope he has success.

Wednesday, 25 June 2008.

Luke arrived late in the evening, after the ballroom dancing had finished. He advise me that he had completed three different searches. All he came up with were minor references to the relevant such as Henri.com - but sorry, no files. He also stated that the hard drive had not only been reformatted but overwritten as well. I gave him a few hundred dollars for his trouble.

I thought he might manage one file or even half a file, but no - nothing. Consequently, I am experiencing a deep let-down feeling at this very moment. Not just for myself, for I will find out what is going on soon enough, but I feel Henri's words would have meant so much to so many.

I've been waiting years now for these files. I felt as though it has been a litany of disasters with no breaks coming my way. I am not depressed but I am definitely experiencing a low emotional state. Hopefully the pall should lift by tomorrow.

Early October, 2008.

By now I have accepted that the files are not going to be retrieved. I don't know why this disaster occurred. I feel Henri, or my Guide, Braida, could have intervened somehow. They could have created scenarios to prevent this disaster from happening. Also, Braida, my Guide, who had previously spoken to me for years - if the files were so important, why not warn me?

I can only conclude that the information given to Guillaume will arrive somehow, someday, by someone, and at the appropriate time. Or are there are other reasons that I am unaware of, why that information has gone missing?

At present, anyone's guess is as good as mine. I intend to make another appointment with Suzy, the medium. That will allow me to conclude this present book; as well it will give Guillaume a chance to offer some explanations. or Braida, or even Henri, any of them might have something to say regarding the missing files.

Monday, 3 November 2008.

Up early, then off to see Suzy, who lives on the North Coast. My appointment was for noon. I spent two hours with her and got everything I came for and more.

Wow! Mind blowing really. I had written down five key questions to ask. During the session, each question was answered without me needing to ask any of them.

Mum and Dad are always there, also our huge pet St Bernard dog that Dad was fond of.

Of course, there was Braida, my Guide. And big surprise! For the first time, Henri, Guillaume's Guide, had arrived on the scene.

Basically, I was advised that both Braida and Henri will join forces to assist me. Apparently, they want me to write down specifically what Henri says - not to add any of my own interpretations.

"Did I have a small tape recorder?" Suzy inquired.

"Several." I replied.

Altogether, a very powerful session. None of my other family or friends who had died during the last two years came through; not my brother, nor even Guillaume, nor any other close friends who had recently dropped off the perch.

I was told by Henri and Braida that the information on the computer was allowed to be lost because of a number of inaccuracies. As well, some information was entirely missing, as Guillaume hadn't written it down. That information will need to be recorded and written down at some future date. Quite a job.

Mentioned for the third time was the sacred Cathar cup, the grail or chalice, which was used in Cathar rituals; those rituals were mainly concerning birth and death. I was informed that the grail is silver and very heavy. It is engraved with the design of the Cathar mandala. To this day it still remains undiscovered.

I was also informed that because of the way it was wrapped in a cloth which has been soaked in an oil extracted from a local tree, it is still in pristine condition.

My tape recorder now contains two hours of information; quite an eventful day. Now it's waiting to see what the future has in store for me.

Hindsight is a wonderful thing. It's now understandable that the information was lost as Henri's remarks weren't set down verbatim. Whether it took place by fate or design, I know not. I do know Guillaume was struggling personally with some of the information that Henri presented, because he told me so. At no point though, did he ever relate to me what philosophic aspects he was internally struggling with.

I presume, Guillaume needing to make logic and sense from some of Henri's discussions, that probably led him to do some occasional revising.

I didn't see Guillaume during the last year of his life, although we conversed on the phone most every week or two. During our phone chats, we made appointment after appointment to meet. Often Guillaume would say, "I have some interesting things to relate, but I want to tell you about them face to face." But it was not to be. He cancelled each appointment we had arranged for one reason or another.

Then Fate intervened; he died quite suddenly. Although he had been ill for years it was still quite a shock, for he seemed to be gathering in both health and strength after recovering from his last operation.

I'm sure in the world of spirit, he and Henri still don't see eye to eye, for Guillaume would insist on rationalising to the 'nth degree, which could be irritating in the extreme.

While I was having my last session with Suzy, she asked me, "Was Henri an angry person?"

I replied I didn't rightly know, but I remembered Guillaume would sometimes say to me, "Henri and I aren't speaking; he is quite upset with me."

Well I'm sure, Guillaume's propensity for rationalisation could try anyone's patience, even that of a saint. Not that I am in any way suggesting sainthood for a good old fashioned heretic like Henri de Nebours.

I have set down in *The Cathar Dialogues*, as best I can as an honest record of that which had transpired over those eventful eight years. Some excerpts of conversations between Guillaume and I weren't included as they have already become too fragmented and submerged for such is the way of memory.

I do feel that the lightness and bluntness contained within the literary style that is Henri's, belies the depth of his subject matter. I continue to gain more understanding, more comprehension, each time I reread *The Cathar Dialogues*. My hope is that they also offer you continuing insights, irrespective of your personal beliefs. For most people, any deductions arrived at from the *Dialogues* will be personal.

As each person's Path is a solitary life's journey, Catharism is but another path to travel by and certainly not a crowded one, for to paraphrase Henri de Nebours, "This is a crusade for the few, not the multitude."

Catharism as a lifestyle however does beckon us with an expected arrival of an inner joy and inner bliss, derived from the awareness of the eventual reunion of one's Divine Spark with a loving Source, rather than the fear of possible damnation in the hereafter for any religious lawbreakers by a vengeful and judgemental Deity..

In this respect, I believe, Cathar beliefs offer greater peace of mind along with tranquility of soul, far exceeding any other philosophy or theology that to date has made us aware of its existence.

It is my ardent wish for those searching souls that *The Cathar Dialogues* and *A Cathar Gnostic Codex*, both assist it readers as salve for the heart and balm for the soul.

Matheus
Johny Bineham

For further information
Google:
Johny Bineham
or
YouTube:
deMontserver
for talks on Catharism and Gnosticism
or
to discuss some Cathar experience,
Please contact me at:
jbbjohny@gmail.com

Addendum D

Glossary

Albigensian   Another term for Cathar; derived from the town of Albi where heretics were numerous, This was the origin of the term 'Albigensian Crusade'

alchemy   Medieval and Renaissance alchemists created complex chemical experiments in their quest to turn base metals into gold. However, mystical alchemy was essentially about the transformation and transmutation of the soul from its sensual base to its higher mystical transcendent self.

apostate   Someone who totally rejects Christianity.

Articifer   A name given to the Light which broke away from The Source to create the material contingent cosmos as we know it.

Auto da Fe   Lit: Act of Faith. Ritual Catholic mass burnings of heretics.

bonhomme   Lit: a good man. How the male *Perfecti* referred to themselves, also as *bon chretiens*, good christians.

bonfemme   Lit: a good woman. It is how the female Perfecti referred to themselves. also as *bon chretiens*, good christians.

Cathars   A Christian Gnostic sect which flourished mainly in the southern Languedoc area of present day France where the Catholic Church unsuccessfully tried to eliminate them during the Albigensian Crusade but later successfully annihilated them through the terror of the Inquisition.

Consolamentum To become a *Perfecti* or *Perfectae*, the candidate had to undergo rigorous training for three years before being inducted as a *Perfecti* after the ritual ceremony, of the *Consolamentum* during which various Scriptural extracts were quoted, in particular, the opening verses of the Gospel of John.

contingency   Uncertainty of occurrence; things that may happen hereafter; subsequent things dependent on an uncertain event.

Dao   The name given the unknown primordial Source by Lao Tze in the *Dao de Jing*.

Deus Vult   Latin: God wills it.

Divine Spark   Our unchanging individuality, our very essence, quite separate to our mind, body and soul.

Domini Canes   'The hounds of God', the Dominicans.

Dualism   The division of something conceptually into two opposed or contrasted aspects. The belief that there are opposing forces of Good and Evil within the universe. The Great (Abrahamic) faiths believe that a good God is in constant opposition to Satan.

Dualists   Many Dualists believe that the world of

spirit and matter was created by a lesser (evil) divinity (God). Other Dualists believe we are Divine Sparks trapped within our material bodies, as well, we have within us Divine Sparks which will ultimately return to an absolute Source, a Creator, that always existed but which is essentially unknown in human terms, contrasting with the personal God, of our likeness, of the Abrahamic Faiths. Christianity, Islam and Judaism are also Dualist in that they have a good God in permanent opposition to the Devil, or Satan.

empirical   Based on, or verified by, observation and/or personal experience.

esoteric   Intended, or likely, to be understood by a small number of people with a specialized knowledge or interest. Esoteric philosophies, or religions, aspire to personal experience to direct their beliefs rather than the exoteric mainstream religions which direct and instruct their followers what to believe.

experiential   Knowledge based on direct personal experience or observation, rather than being accepted or believed on the basis of another's teaching or belief.

exoteric   Beliefs,   teachings,   doctrines   intended for, or likely to be understood by, the general public.

excommunication   Meaning 'no longer in communion'. Excommunication was used as spiritual punishment of a person or group. As well as excommunication the church culd also impose banishment, shunning or shaming.

Gnostic   A person who follows none but their very own esoteric and experiential philosophic path to gain understanding into the who, what and why of actual mystical reality rather than some 'religious truth'.

The Gnostic aspires to gain esoteric knowledge, gnosis, to gain a direct, mystical and personal personal connection with the Divine.

Gnosticism   This is a broad term covering an esoteric philosophy which believes that the origin of all things is an impersonal creator, the Source, which always was. From this Source each of us has a Divine Spark that yearns to and which will ultimately return to the Source after a necessary cycle of reincarnations. Gnosticism, as a philosophy, has influenced many beliefs especially Christianity, Islam and Judaism.

Hesychasm   A method of meditation contemplating silence emanating form the heart rather than the mind. From the Greek hesychia meaning stillnsss, quietness.

Manisola   The Cathar ritual of the laying of hands.

Mithraism   The God of light, truth and honour. the central figure of the Cult of Mithraism which was, probably of Persian origin. He was also associated with merchants and the protection of warriors, so it was the primary religion of the Roman Legionairres of the later empire. It was the main rival to Christianity for the first three centuries AD.

Pantheism   Identifying God with the universe, or regarding the universe as a manifestation of God. The worshipping or tolerance of all gods.

Perfect   Latin perfectus, was the name given to them by St. bernatrd of Clairvaux, meaning the 'perfect heretic' although he also called the Cathars a 'Godly people'. The were also known as *Perfecti*, *Parafait*, (female *Perfectae*, {*Parfaite*) though they referred to themselves as *bonhommes*, the good people. The Cathar equivalent of priests, they were austere black-robed ascetics who were the heart and soul of the Cathar movement. Bogomilism also had their Perfects.

Source   The origin, the Source of all, the absolute of Absolutes, the'being present'.ultimate cosmic reality, the One behind and beyond everything that is within and without of existence, the ineffable One that is beyond human comprehension or meaningful description. Even so, pure unconditional love emanates from The Source for everybody and everything everywhere.

Telesti   The early Gnostics also termed themselves, the *Telesti*, 'We who are aimed', 'We with the true aim'. The actual term Gnostics was meant originally as a denigratory term for, 'know-it-alls'. It is ironic, because the term stuck and they eventually became known as Gnostics. Similarly as *Perfectus* 'being perfect', was a term of derision by the Church for the Cathars. but terms stick to become accepted over time creating acceptance rather than the derision that was first intended.

syncretism   The amalgamation or the attempt to amalgamate the differences between religions, cultures, or varied schools of thought.

Guillaume de Mirepoix, who was a liege if the MIrepoix family in Languedoc some seven hundred years ago. Guillaume and I were burnt at the stake by the Catholic Church with more than two hundred others at Montsegur on 16 March 1244.

 In this current lifetime he was Jim (Paul) Callaghan, ex-Korean War sniper; ex-Trappist monk; ex-industrial chemist and Itinerant actor.

 He was my good friend, though one who looked after his mind more than his body. His spirit Guide Henri de Nebours tried to assist but to no avail during their many duels of their minds.

 Guillaume was born at Bathurst, New South Wales, on the 27th August 1931 and died in Sydney 8th January 2007 but not before privately acknowledging his long lost Cathar faith.

Al cap des set ans vedrego le laurel

Other books by johny bineham

A CATHAR Codex
A concise summation of the dialogues between Henri de Nebours
and Guillaume de Mirepoix

WEDDINGS
A Total Guide

JOKE BOOK
What A Laugh

THREE WARS A SOLDIER
A Lively Half A Life

THE DESTRUCTION OF CITY TATTERSALLS
By Tweedledum And Tweedledee

You can view my Cathar videos on my YouTube channel: **deMontserver,**
which generally concern Gnostic philosophy and Catharism.

THE CATHAR DIALOGUES

Recommended reading for those interested in Catharism.

. Dr Arthur Guirdham's books about a group reincarnation in the south of England. *The Cathars and Reincarnation* and *We Are One Another* are two books of a series.

. For a comprehensive well-told history of Medieval Catharism, *The Massacre of Montsegur* by Zoe Oldenburg.

. For the origins of European Catharism, *The Medieval Manichee* by Steven Runciman.

. *The Journey Of Souls* and *The Destiny Of Souls* by Michael Newton Ph.D., are not merely about past life regressions but that period of time in the world of spirit immediately after death but before their next reincarnating. Invariably at death each soul is met by their spirit Guide without exception, as well, the returning souls in every case refer to the Creator as The Source. Both books, though originating from an entirely different and contemporary origin, validate in many ways how Henri de Nebours describes The Source in *The Cathar Dialogues*.

. Lao Tse's Chinese classic the *Dao de Jing* is about nature being the teacher and about seeking simplicity in all things. I was advised if that if the words The Source were substituted for Dao in the *Dao de Jing,* it could be regarded as a Cathar philosophic manual.

. Without experiencing confusion from the many and varied ancient Gnostic writings, *The Gospel of St. Thomas* gives a fair insight into the world of early Christian Gnostic's thinking, as well as most likely being the earliest gospel written, some say around 50 years after the death of Christ.

Made in United States
Troutdale, OR
07/13/2023

11176520R00084